Mariel Irvine is a solicitor and qualified data protection practitioner. She was a partner in an insurance litigation firm in the City before founding her firm twenty years ago. This is her third legal textbook.

She acts as an external Data Protection Officer for companies and advises businesses in a number of different sectors, particularly when taking over other companies, setting up and merging websites and obtaining consent for marketing from customers. She provides data protection training in both the private and public sector.

A Practical Guide to Enforcing Data Protection Rights and Compensation for Data Breaches

A Practical Guide to Enforcing Data Protection Rights and Compensation for Data Breaches

Mariel Irvine

Law Brief Publishing

Published 2023 by Law Brief Publishing, an imprint of Law Brief Publishing Ltd
30 The Parks
Minehead
Somerset
TA24 8BT

www.lawbriefpublishing.com

Paperback: 978-1-914608-40-7

For David

PREFACE

My interest in data protection began when my longest standing client instructed me to defend proceedings claiming for compensation for a data breach and infringement of the claimant's article 8 right to privacy. The claimant was in a safety critical role and had lost his job when his employer was notified that he had initially failed a drugs test. In successfully defending the case I saw the-importance of this area of the law.

Since then, technology has developed. Its use has filtered into so many areas of daily life. Data protection now covers facial recognition and artificial intelligence, and scraping the internet for information about individuals for fraudulent purposes. Even where an organisation has done what it can to secure its data any breach, no matter how minor, can badly damage its reputation.

This book is designed to be a comprehensive point of reference for organisations and individuals who need to understand and apply the legislative, procedural and policy provisions that are relevant to enforcement.

The applicable law is dated 2 May 2023.

Mariel Irvine
May 2023

CONTENTS

CHAPTER ONE

INTRODUCTION

Data protection law is a developing area of increasing importance. It protects the individual's right to privacy by giving them rights over their personal information, and restricting the way organisations can use this information. It covers a broad spectrum of emotive topics including the media's hounding of celebrities, cold calling the vulnerable, and the harvesting and sale of personal information following security breaches. The law in this area would be ineffective without enforcement.

This book considers the enforcement of data protection rights, including compensation for data breaches, from both the individual's and organisation's points of view. They are obviously two sides of the same coin: complaints to the regulator about data breaches by organisations may trigger enforcement action against the organisation.

Since the General Data Protection Regulation ("GDPR") came into force on 25 May 2018, the Information Commissioner has fined large organisations millions of pounds for data security breaches. However, most fines concern breaches of the Privacy and Electronic Communications Regulations 2003 (PECR) which govern electronic communications from organisations to individuals, including marketing. Although the E-Privacy Regulation was planned to be implemented alongside the GDPR, and would have triggered changes to PECR before Brexit, the Regulation is not yet in force. The maximum fine for breaches of PECR remains £500,000. The provisions of PECR are not considered in this book, which focuses specifically on data protection enforcement under the UK GDPR and Data Protection Act 2018.

When opening the Data Protection Practitioner's Conference in July 2022the Information Commissioner, John Edwards, confirmed he had challenged his team to save business at least £100 million in the next three years. That would be achieved by offering greater certainty in what the law required, coupled with a predictable approach to enforcement action that allowed businesses to invest and innovate with confidence. The same year he decided to reduce the number of fines imposed on organisations in the public sector with the justification that fines divert funds that would be better used by the organisation to fulfil its public function for the public benefit.

Large fines against big companies attract much publicity and may give individuals the mistaken impression that they, too, can recover similar amounts for the data breaches they have suffered. In fact the compensation awarded by the courts tends to be relatively low in individual cases, to the extent that it may be uneconomic to issue proceedings. Often it is only where a breach affects thousands of data subjects, as was the case with the British Airways breach of 2018 for example, that the outlay is likely to be significant. Such cases tend to settle in order to limit legal costs.

A relatively recent data breach case which went to trial and was then appealed to the Supreme Court involved Morrisons supermarket.[1] Morrisons argued they were not vicariously liable for a serious security breach of personal information belonging to thousands of staff, which had been perpetrated by a disgruntled employee. He was in prison for offences related to the breach. A Group Litigation Order was made and thousands of employees joined proceedings in the High Court against the supermarket chain. They walked away with nothing when the Supreme Court decided Morrisons were not vicariously liable for the criminal actions of the employee. His acts had not been sufficiently connected to his employment, and he had been on a frolic of his own.

In order to try and avoid the administrative costs involved with Group Litigation Orders, there have been a number of unsuccessful attempts to

1 *WM Morrisons Supermarkets plc (Appellant) v Various Claimants (Respondent)* [2020] UKSC 12

bring representative actions on behalf of individuals affected by data breaches who have not "opted in", and so are not formally joined as parties to the proceedings. The Safari Workaround Litigation against Google is a crucial example.[2] The Supreme Court was clear that individuals must not only be represented but joined to the proceedings in order to recover compensation. The requirements of causation and proof of damage in individual cases continue to apply. Perhaps a representative action based on alternative causes of action in privacy law, such as misuse of private information, might be successful?

After only two and half years, the GDPR was replaced by the UK GDPR on 1 January 2021, the day after the United Kingdom finally left the European Union. The UK GDPR incorporates the GDPR as it was on 31 December 2020 into domestic law, with necessary amendments identified in a Keeling schedule. Part 2 of the Data Protection Act 2018 supplements and refines the UK GDPR. Both pieces of legislation should be considered together

As yet, there has been no divergence of significance between the UK and EU versions of the GDPR, perhaps partly because too great a divergence might threaten the European Commission's adequacy assessment for transfers of personal data to the UK. The current adequacy decision is likely to last until 27 June 2025. However, when in 2022 the Government withdrew a new bill which would have made some significant amendments to the 2018 Act, it was said this was done so as to enable it to make more far reaching alterations to data protection legislation in future.

The enforcement rights covered in this book are summarised below:-

1. An individual has the right to lodge a complaint with the Information Commissioner if they consider that the processing

---

2 *Lloyd (Respondent) v Google LLC (Appellant)* [2021] UKSC 50

of personal data relating to them infringes the requirements of the UK GDPR and the Data Protection Act 2018.[3]

2. If the Commissioner does not handle the complaint or does not inform the data subject of its progress or the outcome within three months the data subject has the right to appeal to the First-tier Tribunal General Regulatory Chamber. [4]

3. An organisation may appeal to the First-tier Tribunal against information and assessment notices, and also enforcement and penalty notices, issued by the Information Commissioner.[5]

4. A data subject whose rights have been infringed as a result of non-compliance with a provision of the UK GDPR when processing their personal data may apply to the court for an order to secure compliance. [6]

5. A data subject, or any other person, who has suffered *material and non-material damage* as a result of an infringement of the Data Protection Act 2018 may claim compensation in the court against the controller or processor for the damage suffered. Damage covers distress as well as financial loss.[7]

The legislation and guidance to which reference is made includes:

- The UK GDPR and Keeling Schedule
- Data Protection Act 2018

---

[3] Article 77 UK GDPR and s165 DPA 18

[4] Article 78 ibid and s166 DPA 18

[5] Section 162 DPA 18

[6] Article 79 UK GDPR and s167 DPA 18

[7] Section 169 DPA 18

- The Tribunal Procedure (First-tier Tribunal) General Regulatory Chamber) Rules 2009
- The Tribunal Procedure (Upper Tribunal) Rules 2008
- Civil Procedure Rules
- The Information Commissioner's Regulatory Action Policy
- The Information Commissioner's Regulatory and Enforcement Activity Policy on Communicating.

CHAPTER TWO

PRELIMINARIES

In order to put enforcement into context, some of data protection law's key concepts and definitions are briefly described in this chapter.

Personal data

Personal data are any information from which a living individual can be identified, either directly or indirectly. [8]They are not limited to names and identification numbers, or to photographs or addresses. They may be a large shoe size, if there is a person in the organisation known to have big feet. Information may become personal data if a person becomes identifiable when data are combined with other information that subsequently comes into the possession of an organisation.

Special category data

These are information revealing an individual's racial or ethnic origin, political opinions, religious or philosophical beliefs, trade union membership, together with genetic and biometric data, health information and data in relation to a person's sex or sexual orientation. A second legitimising condition is required in order to process this category of personal data lawfully.[9]

8 Article 4 (1) UK GDPR

9 Article 9 ibid

Special purposes

The *special purposes* are journalism, academic, artistic and/or literary. Personal data processed for these purposes is protected from enforcement procedures against controllers and processors in a number of respects.

The Information Commissioner may make a written determination that personal data is not being processed only for special purposes or that it is not being processed with a view to the publication of journalistic, academic, artistic or literary material which has not previously been published by the controller. [10] Where such a determination is made and notice given of it to the controller and processor setting out their rights of appeal, the various restrictions on enforcement action may not apply. A controller or processor may appeal against such a determination to the First-tier Tribunal (General Regulatory Chamber) under section 162 (4) Data Protection Act 2018.

Special purposes proceedings refers to legal proceedings against a controller or processor which *relate wholly or partly to personal data processed for the special purposes.* An individual who is a party or prospective party to such proceedings may apply to the Commissioner for assistance. [11] Where proceedings concern the processing of personal data for special purposes alone, or for the publication of material for special purposes which has not previously been published by the controller the court must stay the proceedings. [12]

---

[10] Section 174 (3) DPA 2018

[11] Section 175 ibid

[12] Section 176 ibid

Data subject

A data subject is an individual whose personal data is processed by a third party.[13]

Processing

Processing covers any activity involving personal data, including holding, storage and destruction. [14] An email in a person's in box which contains personal data will fall within the definition of processing. The Information Commissioner confirms it is difficult to imagine an activity involving personal data that does not fall within the definition of processing.

Data controller

A data controller decides the why and the how of personal data processing. [15]It decides why it needs to collect personal data and how to process it. A controller may be a sole trader, a partnership, a private or public limited company, or a large multi-national organisation.

Data processor

A data processor processes personal data in accordance with the written instructions of the data controller. [16]

---

[13] Article 4 (1) UK GDPR

[14] Article 4 (2) ibid

[15] Article 4 (7) ibid

[16] Article 4 (8) ibid

Legitimising conditions

The UK GDPR does not apply to the processing of personal data *in the course of a purely personal or household activity* [17]. Nor does it apply to the processing of personal data by a competent authority for law enforcement purposes or to intelligence services processing. [18]

Otherwise the UK GDPR applies and the processing of personal data is unlawful unless a legitimising condition, or lawful basis, applies. Legitimising conditions include processing carried out to fulfil a contract, processing carried out with consent and processing which is in the legitimate interests of a business. [19]

Special category data, such as health information, requires an additional legitimising condition such as explicit consent or engagement in legal claims. [20]

The seven data protection principles

Where there is a lawful basis for processing personal data, the processing must be carried out in accordance with the principles and conditions of the UK GDPR and Data Protection Act 2018.

The seven data protection principles[21] are listed below:

- Lawfulness, fairness and transparency;

---

17 Article 2 (a) ibid

18 Article 2 (b) and (c) ibid

19 Article 6 ibid

20 Article 9 ibid

21 Article 5 UK GDPR

- Purpose limitation;
- Data minimisation;
- Data accuracy;
- Storage limitation;
- Integrity confidentiality and security;
- Accountability.

Breach of these principles may trigger enforcement action, either at the instigation of the data subject or at the instigation of the Information Commissioner. The Commissioner targets industry sectors in order to ensure that data is being processed lawfully.

Security

Data controllers and processors must implement appropriate technical and organisational measures to ensure a level of security appropriate to the risk. This is a free standing security obligation at Article 32 UK GDPR, in addition to the security obligation included in the data protection principles under Article 5, listed above.

Data breach

A data breach is a breach of security which leads to *the accidental or unlawful destruction, loss, alteration, unauthorised disclosure of, or access to, personal data transmitted, stored or otherwise processed.* [22] It is a very broad

[22] Article 4 (12) ibid

definition which covers leaving files in taxis and losing unencrypted USB sticks in the post.

Notification of personal data breaches

When a personal data breach occurs, the controller has an obligation[23] to notify the Information Commissioner without undue delay and not later than 72 hours after becoming aware of it, if possible. If notification is not made within 72 hours reasons must be given for the delay.

If the breach is *unlikely to result in a risk for the rights and freedoms of natural persons* the controller is not required to notify the Commissioner.

Where there is a *high risk to the rights and freedoms of natural persons,* the controller must not only notify the controller but communicate the data breach to the data subject without undue delay.[24]

Rights of data subjects

The rights of data subjects over their personal data processed by others are contained in Chapter 3 of the UK GDPR, as summarised below.

- Right to be informed about the processing of their personal data;
- Right of access to personal data by means of a subject access request;
- Right to rectification of inaccurate data,

---

[23] Article 33 ibid

[24] Article 34 ibid

- Right to erasure, otherwise known as the right to be forgotten;

- Right to restrict the processing of personal data in certain circumstances;

- Right to data portability or to transfer personal data from the IT system of one organisation directly to another;

- Right to object to processing and also the right to object to direct marketing;

- Rights in relation to automated decision making and profiling.

Controllers have one month to respond to data subject requests to exercise these rights, with a long stop deadline of three months where the request is complex or there are multiple requests.[25] A controller should acknowledge the request and give a reason for requiring any extension within one month of receipt of the request.

Section 149 (2) Data Protection Act 2018

Section 149(2) describes breaches of the data protection legislation which may trigger an enforcement notice. They include breaches of:

- the data protection principles;

- the rights of data subjects;

- the obligations of controllers and processors; and

- the requirements to communicate data beaches.

25 Article 12 UK GDPR

Other parts of the Act refer to this subsection as providing the basis for other enforcement methods, such as information and assessment notices, penalty notices and also the issuing of warrants.

Data Protection Legislation

Data protection legislation means the UK GDPR, the Data Protection Act 2018 and regulations made under it and *regulations made under section 2 (2) European Communities Act 1972 which relate to the EU GDPR or the Law Enforcement Directive.* [26]

[26] Section 3 (9) DPA 2018

CHAPTER THREE

ENFORCEMENT AGAINST THE INFORMATION COMMISSIONER

Information Commissioner

John Edwards was appointed Information Commissioner in December 2021. As such he is the regulator responsible for data protection in the United Kingdom.

He:-

- monitors and enforces compliance with the UK GDPR and Data Protection Act 2018;
- promotes awareness among data controllers and processors of their obligations under data protection legislation;
- maintains a register of data controllers and levies a registration fee;
- provides information to data subjects about their information rights when they request it;
- handles and investigates complaints lodged by data subjects;
- conducts investigations and takes enforcement action, if necessary; and
- in extreme cases, prosecutes companies that misuse data.

The Information Commissioner's Office (ICO) often works with other regulators and agencies in order to deliver its enforcement remit, such as with the National Crime Agency, the Financial Conduct Authority and the Competition and Markets Authority. Its jurisdiction may overlap with theirs and the agencies may undertake joint regulatory or investigative work so as to minimise duplication. Various memoranda of understanding with these and other organisations are published on the ICO's website.

The website is an excellent resource. The information it provides includes guidance and policies for specific industry sectors, together with details of recent enforcement activity. It repays regular review.

Complaints to the Commissioner

The initial and most cost-effective avenue of redress for an individual who considers there has been an infringement of their rights under the data protection legislation is to lodge a complaint with the Information Commissioner [27]. Where, for example, a data subject requests access to their personal data and suspects that full access has not been given, they may complain to the Commissioner that there has been a breach of their right of access.

There is no requirement that the belief in the infringement be reasonable. Section 165 (2) Data Protection Act 2018 provides:-

> *A data subject may make a complaint to the Commissioner if the data subject considers that, in connection with personal data relating to him or her, there is an infringement ....*

[27] Section165 DPA 2018 and Article 77 (1)UK GDPR

However the Commissioner is required to investigate complaints only *to the extent appropriate* and so has some discretion where complaints appear to be lacking in substance. [28]

Such complaints, together with:- (a) reports of personal data breaches from controllers to the Commissioner [29] and (b) the Commissioner's concerns about data protection compliance in particular industry sectors, are the usual triggers for formal investigations and enforcement action by the regulator. At the time of writing, the Commissioner is investigating compliance in the direct marketing data broking sector.

Steps to take before complaining to the Comissioner

The ICO advises those who wish to make a formal complaint to take the following steps first:-

1. Complain directly to the organisation;

2. Chase the organisation if there is no response in 28 days;

3. Ask for clarification if the response is unclear.

The Commissioner requires that any complaint should be lodged with the ICO within three months of the person's *last contact with the organisation*. This is broadly worded and probably includes contact made by the complainant with the organisation, such as a chasing email, as well as contact from the organisation itself.

When making a complaint the data subject is advised to produce evidence of the earlier complaint to the organisation and its response, together with any other evidence that is relevant.. The more information

---

28 Section 165 (5) (a) DPA 2018

29 Article 33 UK GDPR

and evidence that is provided, the speedier the ICO should be in providing an outcome.

ICO response to complaint

The ICO allocates the complaint to a case officer whom the Commissioner describes as weighing up the *facts of what has happened fairly and impartially.* They may ask both the complainant and the organisation for more information before providing an outcome. There is no time limit for providing an outcome, although in the absence of an outcome, the ICO must keep the complainant informed of progress by providing an update within three months of receiving complaint.

Under section 165 (4) Data Protection Act 2018, when he receives a complaint the Commissioner must:-

(a) take appropriate steps to respond to the complaint,

(b) inform the complainant of the outcome of the complaint,

(c) inform the complainant of their rights under section 166, and

(d) if asked to do so by the complainant, provide the complainant with further information about how to pursue the complaint.

Section 165 (5) defines *appropriate steps* as including –

(a) *investigating the subject matter of the complaint, to the extent appropriate, and*

(b) *informing the complainant about the progress of the complaint, including about whether further investigation or co-ordination with another supervisory authority or foreign designated authority is necessary.*

The possible outcomes to a complaint are listed on the ICO website as follows:-

- Notifying the organisation that they have done nothing wrong and there has been no infringement of the law;

- Logging the complaint and using it for intelligence in order to help build a picture of an organisation's information rights practices; (See *Delo* below.)

- Asking the organisation to do more work to resolve the complaint or explain their position more clearly. This could mean asking the organisation to provide information or correct inaccuracies;

- Making recommendations to the organisation on how they can improve their information rights practices. This can include asking an organisation to review their policies or procedures, guidance or standards.

Regulatory action is reserved for the most serious cases. The ICO confirms: *We do not normally take regulatory action for individual complaints as we want organisations to comply with the law without us using our formal powers…However, even if we don't take action, we will keep a record of the complaint to help us to build up a picture of how well an organisation is following the law.*

When complaining, some individuals mistakenly assume that the Commissioner can award them compensation, although it has no power to do so.

Enforcement against commissioner

Application to the First Tier Tribunal

If the case officer fails to comply with the requirements of section 165 (above) the data subject may make an application under section 166 Data Protection Act 2018 to the First-tier Tribunal (General Regulatory Chamber) ("the Tribunal") for an order requiring the Information Commissioner to comply.[30] An appeal lies from the Tribunal to the Upper Tribunal (Administrative Appeals Chamber). The procedure in both chambers is examined in Chapter 8.

Many of the applications to the Tribunal against the Information Commissioner concern section 166 and are made in the mistaken belief that it provides an avenue for appealing against the the Commissioner's substantive decision in response to a complaint. In fact the section allows appeals against the ICO's procedural failure to report on progress or provide an outcome. The Tribunal may order the Commissioner to inform the complainant of the outcome of the complaint within a specified period. It may also order the Commissioner to conclude an investigation within a specified period.[31]

Section 166 (1) provides a remedy where the Commissioner: –

> *(a) fails to take appropriate steps to respond to the complaint,*
>
> *(b) fails to provide the complainant with information about progress on the complaint, or of the outcome of the complaint, before the end of the period of 3 months beginning when the Commissioner received the complaint, or*

---

[30] Section 166 DPA 2018

[31] Section 166 (3) ibid

> *(c) if the Commissioner's consideration of the complaint is not concluded during that period, fails to provide the complainant with such information during a subsequent period of 3 months.*

In response to these failings a data subject may apply to the Tribunal under section 166 (2) for an order requiring the Commissioner:

> *(a) to take appropriate steps to respond to the complaint, or*
>
> *(b) to inform the complainant of progress on the complaint, or of the outcome of the complaint, within a period specified in the order.*

The ICO generally rectifies its failures on receipt of an application. Once an outcome is provided the application to the Tribunal becomes academic. There is no longer any failure and the application is struck out.[32]

In *Killock & Veale v the Information Commissioner* [2021] UKUT 299 (AAC) the Upper Tribunal (UT) confirmed that *the Tribunal has no power to deal with the merits of the complaint or its outcome.* At paragraph 76 of its judgement it explained:

> *The Commissioner is the expert regulator. She is the best person to consider the merits of a complaint and to reach a conclusion as to its outcome. In so far as the Commissioner's regulatory judgements would not and cannot be matched by expertise in the Tribunal, it is readily comprehensible that Parliament has not provided a remedy in the Tribunal in relation to the merits of complaints…*

---

[32] Rule 8 *The Tribunal Procedure (First-tier Tribunal) (General Regulatory Chamber) Rules 2009*

The Commissioner was best placed to decide what investigations she should undertake into any particular issue and how she should conduct those investigations. She could take into account her regulatory priorities, other investigations she was conducting in the same area and how to deploy her limited resources most effectively. [33]

Most importantly:

> *... s 166 is a forward looking provision, concerned with remedying ongoing procedural defects that stand in the way of a timely resolution of a complaint. The Tribunal is tasked with specifying appropriate "steps to respond" and not with assessing the appropriateness of a response that has already been given ... We do not rule out circumstances in which a complainant, having received an outcome to his or her complaint under section 165 (b), may ask the Tribunal to wind back the clock and to make an order for an appropriate step to be taken in response to a complaint under s 166 (2) (a).* ***However, should that happen the Tribunal will cast a critical eye to assure itself that the complainant is not using the s 166 process to achieve a different complaint outcome.*** [Emphasis added.][34]

However, the Upper Tribunal confirmed that the Commissioner's view on what *steps* were appropriate was not decisive:. *....the language of sections 165 and 166 is objective in that it does not suggest that an investigative step in response to a complaint is appropriate because the Commissioner thinks it is appropriate: her view will not be decisive...*[35]The Tribunal gave a very narrow example of when the Tribunal might

[33] Paragraphs 85 and 86, *Killock & Veale v Information Commissioner* 2021] UKUT 299 (AAC)

[34] Paragraph 87 ibid

[35] Paragraph 84 ibid

substitute its own decision for the Commissioner's: where a response should be given in braille.

The case of *EW v Information Commissioner*, which was heard alongside *Killock*, concerned the Commissioner's failure to take appropriate steps. The Upper Tribunal found that she had misconstrued and misapplied her own Service Standards. She had refused to investigate a complaint because it was made more than three months after the complainant's last contact with the organisation, although her Service Standards merely suggested that complaints be made within three months of the last contact. The Upper Tribunal made this determination at paragraph 166:

> *In our judgment, by misconstruing and misapplying her own Service Standards, and thereby simply declining to investigate the complaints at all, the Commissioner did not take such steps as were appropriate to respond to the complaints.*

In the more recent case of *Osifeso v ICO* [2022] UKUR 146 (AAC) the data subject made an application to the Tribunal on a procedural point, concerning the appropriate steps for the ICO to take to investigate her complaint. The central issue was whether s 166 (2) was wide enough to allow the Tribunal to consider, not the merits of the decision, *but the appropriateness of the investigative steps that lead to it.* At paragraph 22 of its judgement the Upper Tribunal referred to *Killock* and perhaps somewhat vaguely and unhelpfully said: *To sum up the degree of judicial oversight appropriate for section 166 applications could be described as relatively light touch but not hands off.* [36]

The Upper Tribunal decided the reality was the Appellant was trying to challenge the substantive outcome of her complaint. Any challenge to the outcome was to be pursued in the High Court by way of judicial review. Alternatively a claim could be made against the data controller in the High Court or county court.

---

[36] Paragraph 22 *Osifeso v Information Commissioner* 2022] UKUT 146 (AAC)

Judicial review

An avenue for reviewing the outcome of a decision reached by the Information Commissioner is by an application for judicial review to the Administrative Court. However, even where such an application is successful, the Commissioner may simply reach the same decision again after remedying any defects found in his decision making process.

The time limit for issuing such proceedings is three months from the decision complained about, and it is imperative that proceedings are issued well before the deadline where that is possible. Before issue a claimant should first submit a formal letter of claim and allow sufficient time for a response so timeis very tight.

In their service standards relating to data protection complaints, the ICO states;

> *Our role is not to investigate or adjudicate on every individual complaint. We are not an ombudsman. But we will consider whether there is an opportunity to improve the practice of the organisations we regulate and we will share our decisions with you.*

Mr Justice Mostyn confirmed the lawfulness of this approach *R (on the application of Delo) v Information Commissioner and another* [2022] EWHC 3046 (Admin)

In that case the claimant issued proceedings for judicial review against the Information Commissioner when he decided not to investigate his complaint about the adequacy of an organisation's disclosure in response to a data subject access request. The Commissioner had simply read the claimant's letter of complaint and the accompanying correspondence before deciding to take no further action. He had made no enquiries of the data controller.

At the same time the claimant issued separate proceedings against the data controller who had failed to provide full access to his personal data. When the controller provided the missing documents in response to the proceedings, the judicial review became academic. Nevertheless, Mr Justice Mostyn decided to determine the case. It was in the public interest to do so as *the core question has not been directly considered in domestic or European case law in the 41 years since the right to data protection came into existence or in the 4 1/2 years since the EU GDPR became part of the law.*[37]

The judge referred to sections 166 (2) and (3) (above) which allow the Tribunal to order the Commissioner to take the steps specified in the order to respond to the complaint. With considerable clarity he explained:

> *In my judgement, this would not extend to telling the Commissioner that he had to reach a conclusive determination on a complaint where the Commissioner had rendered an outcome of no further action without reaching a conclusive determination. This is because s 166 by its terms applies only where the claim is pending and has not reached the outcome stage. It applies only to alleged deficiencies in procedural steps along the way and clearly does not apply to a merits-based outcome decision.*[38]

He decided that:

> *The Commissioner was under no obligation either to seek further materials from Wise* (the data controller] *or to reach a conclusive determination as to whether, or not, Wise had complied with its data protection obligations. It was sufficient*

[37] Paragraph 122, *R (on the application of Delo) v Information Commissioner*, [2022] EWHC 3046 (Admin)

[38] Paragraph 128 ibid

> *for him to conclude on the basis of the available information that it appeared likely that Wise had so complied.*
>
> *The Commissioner dealt with the complaints in his capacity as an expert Regulator in accordance with the legal requirements. He did so to the letter. There is no warrant for saying either that he failed as a matter of fact to determine the complaints; or that he handled them in violation of the law; or that his decision making process left out of account material matters, or took into account irrelevant matters, or was otherwise irrational. These criticisms all stem from the false argument....that it is the obligation of the Commissioner in every case where a complaint is made, to investigate to the extent necessary to enable him to reach a conclusive determination.* [39]

The claimant appealed. At the time of writing the judgement of the Court of Appeal has not been handed down.

<u>Complaints to the ICO and to the Parliamentary and Health Service Ombudsman</u>

The Parliamentary and Health Service Ombudsman considers complaints made about the Information Commissioner. It recommends that the complainant complain first to himand give him the opportunity to put things right.

The ICO provides aprocedure for making such complaints . If a complainant disagrees with the outcome of a complaint about data processing, they should contact the ICO within three months for consideration under the Commissioner's case review process.

The ICO will acknowledge the complaint within 14 days and aim to respond in full within 30 days. In complex cases the ICO may ask the

[39] Paragraph 143 ibid

complainant to agree the scope of the complaint. If the Commissioner cannot issue a response within 30 days he will provide regular updates and a target date by which he aims to issue the response. A response to complex cases should be issued in six weeks. [40]

Complaints to the Ombudsman must be made to an MP within a year of when the complainant became aware of the problem. The MP then needs to pass the complaint to the Ombudsman. The Ombudsman may not investigate a complaint if the complainant has or had the option to issue proceedings in a court or tribunal. It says on its website:

> *If we can see that there is (or was) a possible legal route to answer your complaint, we will talk to you to get a detailed understanding of your concerns and what you want to happen. We will make sure we take into account factors such as how much it might cost you to take legal action, and how long it might take.*
>
> *If it looks to us like legal action would fully answer your concerns, or be able to give you all the results you are looking for, we may decide this is a better option for you.*

The Ombudsman may make a recommendation to the Information Commissioner to put matters right. It cannot compel an organisation to put things right or order it to pay compensation.

---

40 www.ico.org/complain about us

CHAPTER FOUR

INFORMATION COMMISSIONER'S REGULATORY ACTION POLICY

Introduction

After the introduction of the GDPR in May 2018, the previous Information Commissioner, Elizabeth Denham, published a refreshed Regulatory Action Policy (RAP) under the ICO's Information Rights Strategic Plan for 2017 to 2021. In this way she fulfilled her obligation, under section 160 (1) Data Protection Act 2018 to provide guidance on how she would exercise her enforcement function. RAP reflects the clear hierarchy of enforcement powers contained in the data protection legislation.

In her forward to the policy, the Commissioner noted that:

- *Organisations should be able to predict how my office will carry out its regulatory activity;*

- *The ICO acts both as a strong defender of individuals' information rights and as an enabler of organisations seeking to use data responsibly and safely;*

- *Those who are subject to ICO regulatory action should be in no doubt that we will pursue failures under the law in a way that is transparent, consistent and proportionate.*

She explained that her policy focusses *on areas of highest risk and most harm and the principles we apply in exercising our powers.*

The same Regulatory Action Policy remains in place, although a new strategic plan was published on 14 July 2022 to cover the years to 2025. The salient provisions of RAP are summarised in this chapter.

Notification of breaches of the data protection legislation

Under Article 33 UK GDPR, a data controller must report a personal data breach to the Information Commissioner *unless it is unlikely to result in a risk to the rights and freedoms of natural persons. Unlikely* is a high threshold to reach . Much will depend on the nature of the personal data affected by the breach.

Where a breach is likely to result in a high risk to the *rights and freedoms of natural persons,* not only the Information Commissioner but data subjects must also be informed [41] of the breach. The notification must be made without undue delay.

No notification is required where:-

- the personal data was rendered unintelligible to any person who was not authorised to access it, such as by encryption, or
- where the controller has subsequently taken measures to reduce the risk so that it is no longer likely to materialise, or
- where notifying the data subject *would involve disproportionate effort,* in which case there should be a general public communication.

Article 33 requires organisations to maintain a record of data breaches which describes the remedial action taken. The record must be made available to the regulator.

[41] Article 34 UK GDPR

Response to breaches of the data protection legislation.

The ICO considers data breaches and other infringements of the data protection legislation on a case by case basis, weighing up the potential harm to individuals and the culpability of any conduct which caused the breach. It tries to ensure transparency, consistency and proportionality.

The Commissioner's website provides information about specific areas he is reviewing. At the time of writing this included work to recover fines he had imposed and investigating the use of data analytics for political purposes. It is advisable for data controllers and processors to monitor the *Actions We've Taken* tab for developments in their industry sector.

ICO objectives and implementation

In carrying out its regulatory functions the ICO has five objectives of which two are directly relevant to enforcement:-[42]

> ***Objective 1***
>
> *To respond swiftly and effectively to breaches of legislation which fall within the ICO's remit, focussing on (i) those involving highly sensitive information, (ii) those adversely affecting large groups of individuals, and/or (iii) those impacting vulnerable individuals.*
>
> ***Objective 2***
>
> *To be effective, proportionate, dissuasive and consistent in our application of sanctions, targeting our most significant powers (i) for organisations and individuals suspected of **repeated or wilful misconduct or serious failures to take proper steps to protect personal data,** and (ii) where formal regulatory action*

[42] Page 6 RAPy

serves as an important deterrent to those who risk non-compliance with the law. (Emphasis added.]

The guidance goes on to explain that the objectives will be implemented as follows:--

- *we will take action proportionately, we will exercise discretion as to when, in what manner, and to what extent enforcement is required;*

- *we will be selective when exercising this discretion, looking at the features and context of each case, as well as applying our resources more broadly to the areas of greatest risk and potential or actual harm to the community;*

- *we will apply our fining and other enforcement powers where they are effective, proportionate and dissuasive (to both the individual or organisation receiving the fine and more generally to those processing personal data);*

Which enforcement activity?

When deciding whether to take enforcement action and, if so, which enforcement action to take from the hierachy, the Commissioner considers the following criteria, which is not an exhaustive list: [43]

- the seriousness of the breach or potential breach;

- the categories of any personal data affected and whether they include special category data;

[43] Page 10 ibid

- the number of data subjects affected and the extent of any physical, mental or financial damage they have suffered;
- the level of privacy intrusion;
- whether the breach concerns security and whether it arises out of a new or is a repeated issue;
- the gravity and duration of the breach;
- whether the organisation or individual involved with the breach is representative of a sector or group which might have similar issues;
- the cost of measures to mitigate the risk, issue or harm;
- the public interest in regulatory action being taken;
- whether another regulator, law enforcement body or competent authority is already taking (or has already taken action) regarding the same matter.

Aggravating and mitigating factors

In addition the ICO may take into account any aggravating or mitigating factors.[44] Aggravating factors include:

- any *intentional, wilful or negligent approach to compliance*;
- ignoring relevant advice, warnings or guidance from the ICO and/or the organisation's Data Protection Officer;

[44] Pages 11 and 12 RAPy

- holding certification from a body accredited under Article 43 and failing to follow the certification requirements;
- a regulatory history of similar issues;
- the vulnerability of individuals affected, particularly by reason of their age or other characteristics protected under the Equality Act 2010;
- the availability of protective or preventative technology;
- any failure or delay in notifying the ICO of the breach or issue (as required by Article 33 UK GDPR);
- any financial benefits obtained or avoided as a result of the breach or issue.

There are also mitigating factors to be taken into account which include:

- actions taken to reduce any damage suffered by individuals;
- following an approved or statutory code of conduct;
- the absence of effective protective or preventative measures and technology;
- early notification to the ICO of the breach or issue.

The Commissioner's enforcement powers

The Commissioner's enforcement powers are contained in Article 58 of the UK GDPR and Part 6 of the Data Protection Act 2028. The UK GDPR divides the ICO's powers into three categories:-

a) Investigative powers;

b) Corrective powers;

c) Authorisation and advisory powers.

This book is concerned with investigative and corrective powers. The Data Protection Act 2018 implements these powers with a system of information notices, assessment notices, enforcement notices and penalty notices.

Investigative powers

Investigative powers include the ability to:

- order the controller and processor to provide information to the ICO;
- carry out investigations by way of data protection audits;
- notify the controller or processor of an alleged infringement of the UK GDPR;
- obtain access to all personal data and information necessary for the performance of the Commissioners tasks;
- obtain access to any premises of the controller and the processor including to any data processing equipment and means of data processing in accordance with domestic law.

Under Article 31 UK GDPR controllers and processors must co-operate with the Commissioner in the performance of his tasks.

Corrective powers

Corrective powers include

- warning a controller or processor that intended processing operations are likely to infringe the provisions of the UK GDPR;
- reprimanding a controller or processor where processing operations have infringed relevant provisions of the UK GDPR;
- ordering a controller or processor to comply with the data subject's request to exercise his or her rights;
- ordering a controller or processor to bring processing operations into compliance with the UK GDPR in a specified manner and within a specified time period;
- ordering a controller to communicate a personal data breach to the data subject;
- ordering the rectification or erasure of personal data or the restriction of processing and the notification of these actions to recipients to whom personal data have been disclosed;
- imposing a ban on processing and suspension of data flows which may send the organisation out of business;
- ordering an administrative fine in addition to or instead of measures referred to in this list;
- ordering the suspension of data flows to a recipient in a third country or to an international organisation.

Publication

According to the ICO's Regulatory and Enforcement Communications Activity Policy, the Commissioner's default position is that it will publish *all formal regulatory outcomes.* These are described as notices, reprimands, recommendations or reports, together with significant decisions and investigations when the outcome is reached. [45] Where appropriate outcomes will also be publicised.

Preliminary enforcement notices and notices of intent are not routinely published.

Avoiding enforcement action

In dealing with the ICO the watchword is to communicate clearly and effectively and update it promptly. . Attempts to hide infringements may result in more severe penalties. When reporting a breach the former Comissioner Elizabeth Denham's advice was to *Tell it all. Tell it fast. And tell the truth.*

It is important to bear in mind that in many cases the Commissioner may decide not to use his corrective powers and instead engage with the organisation responsible for the non- compliance. In appropriate cases an undertaking may be agreed to prevent future non-compliance.

[45] See page 5 of the policy

CHAPTER FIVE

COMMISSIONER'S INVESTIGATIVE POWERS: INFORMATION AND ASSESSMENT NOTICES: WARRANTS TO ENTER PREMISES

Introduction

The previous chapter reviews the Regulatory Action Policy in which the ICO provides statutory guidance on when the Commissioner will use his investigative powers to serve information and assessment notices.

These powers are provided by Article 58 UK GDPR under which the ICO can order a data controller and processor to provide *any information it requires for the performance of its tasks.* [46] The Commissioner may carry out data protection audits and obtain access to *all personal data and to all information necessary.* [47] He may also obtain access to premises and data processing equipment. [48]

Part 6 Data Protection Act 2018, contains the mechanism for enforcement of these powers.

---

[46] Article 58 (1) (a)

[47] Article 58 (1) (e)

[48] Article 58 (1) (f)

Information notices

Information notices are formal requests under section 142 Data Protection Act 2018 for information the Commissioner reasonably requires to assist him. They may also be served as part of any investigation into suspected breaches of the data protection legislation or into suspected criminal offences under the Data Protection Act 2018.

In deciding whether to issue an information notice, the Commissioner will consider whether a notice is appropriate and proportionate in the circumstances. This will involve reviewing the risk of harm to individuals and the level of intrusion into their privacy as a result of the events under investigation, together with consideration of the general public interest. Two practical criteria are also weighed in the balance when deciding whether to serve a notice: the benefit of having the information by a given deadline, and the greater likelihood that the information provided will be accurate since deliberately or recklessly making a false statement in response to a notice is a criminal offence.[49]

Section 142 contains detailed mandatory provisions. The notice must state its purpose and whether it is to assist the Commissioner with investigating suspected failures of controllers or processors to comply with (a) the seven data protection principles or (b) with the data subject's rights or (c) with their obligations as a controller or processor or (d) with the requirement to communicate a personal data breach to the Commissioner or data subject or (e) with the principles for transfers of personal data to third countries.[50] The notice must also provide an explanation of why this information is needed [51].

It must include a warning about the consequences of failing to comply and the recipient's rights of appeal to the First Tier Tribunal (General

[49] Section 144 DPA 2018

[50] Sections 142 (a) and 149 (2) DPA 2018

[51] Section 142 (b) ibid

Regulatory Chamber) under sections 162 and 164 Data Protection Act 2018 (see Chapter 8 for the Tribunal's procedural rules).

A notice *may*, but is not required to, give a description of the information sought, and also specify the form in which it is to be provided, together with the place where it is to be provided, and also a time limit for doing so. Requests for information may be in the form of questions, as well as requests for identified documents or categories of documents.

The Commissioner may cancel an information notice by giving written notice to the person to whom it was given. [52]

Any deadline provided for compliance must not be less than the 28 day deadline for lodging an appeal. If an appeal is lodged the information need not be provided until the appeal is determined. [53]

Any notice requires careful scrutiny on its face in order to check its legality and decide whether to lodge an appeal. If either the notice or decision to issue the notice is unlawful, or any discretion exercised by the Commissioner should have been exercised differently[54], the Tribunal will allow an appeal or substitute another notice or decision which the Commissioner could have given.

Urgent information notices

If an information notice states that the information is required urgently, giving reasons for this [55], the deadline for compliance may be shorter than

52 Section 142 (8) ibid

53 Sub sections 142 (5) and (6) ibid

54 Section 163 ibid

55 Section 142 (7) ibid

the deadline for an appeal. However it should not be less than 24 hours from receipt of the notice.[56]

When deciding whether he requires the information urgently, the Commissioner *considers whether urgent investigation may prevent or limit the risk of serious harm to individuals or serious intrusion into their privacy. For example requesting an urgent report on a serious data security breach in order for the ICO to advise the controller on and validate appropriate notification to data subjects and appropriate mitigation of the breach.*[57]He also considers the likelihood that urgent investigation may prevent the destruction and alteration of evidence.

In addition he weighs up the impact of a notice on the recipient. He reviews the extent of the information request, the additional burden on the recipient in having to comply urgently, and also the impact on the rights of the recipient if the information is obtained before any appeal is heard by the Information Tribunal. The comparative effectiveness of the Commissioner's other investigatory powers will also be taken into account.[58]

A recipient may appeal to the Tribunal not only against the decision to issue an urgent information notice but also against the deadline.[59]

Restrictions on information notices

Some personal data processing falls outside the scope of information notices.

---

56 Section 142 (7) ibid

57 See pages 15 and 16 RAP

58 See pages 15 and 16 RAPy

59 Section 164 DPA 2018

Processing of personal data for special purposes

The processing of personal data for *special purposes* (see Chapter 2 for a definition) may not be included in a notice .

In order to bypass this provision, the Commissioner may make a written determination under section 174 Data Protection Act 2018 that the processing is not only for special purposes or that the personal data is not being processed with a view to the publication of material which has not previously been published by the controller. When such a determination is made the restriction does not apply.

Neither does the restriction apply where the Commissioner has reasonable grounds to suspect that a written determination could be made and he requires access to the personal data processed for special purpose for the purposes of making such a determination. [60]

The Commissioner must give written notice of any determination to the controller and the processor together with information about rights of appeal. The determination does not come into effect until the 28-day deadline for an appeal has passed or the avenues of appeal have been exhausted.

Privilege

In an unusual provision, privileged personal data is protected from disclosure, so long as it does not concern the data protection legislation.[61]

---

60 Section 143 (1) (b) ibid

61 Section 143 (3) and (4) ibid

Evidence of the commission of an offence

There is no requirement to provide the Commissioner with information that might expose the person providing the information to proceedings for the commission of an offence. However the protection does not extend to an offence under the Data Protection Act 2018 or to offences under section 5 Perjury Act 1911 (false statements made otherwise than on oath).

Criminal offences

It is an offence for a person to make a false statement in response to an information notice either intentionally or recklessly. [62]

Under section 148 Data Protection Act 2018, it is an offence to destroy or falsify information and documents with the intention of preventing the Commissioner from viewing or being provided with the material. It is defence to prove that the destruction, falsification etc would have occurred irrespective of the notice.

Application for information order

Where there is no response to a notice, the Regulatory Action Policy confirms the Commissioner will promptly apply to the court for an information order under section 145 Data Protection Act 2018. Any order must specify a deadline for providing information. [63]

[62] Section 144 ibid

[63] Section 145 DPA 2018

Publication

The ICO's Communicating our Regulatory and Enforcement Activity Policy confirms the Commissioner is likely to publicise information notices, urgent information notices or court orders for compliance with an information notice if[64]:

- they are in the public domain;
- an update is expected or the ICO needs to show it has taken action; or
- if it helps the ICO's investigation.

However, the time of writing information notices are not published on the page devoted to enforcement action on the ICO website.

Assessment notices

Assessment notices are designed to allow the Commissioner to investigate whether a data controller or processor is complying with the data protection legislation. In order to achieve this they allow him to gain access to premises and equipment so that he can inspect and examine documents and data processing activities[65] and interview individuals concerned with the processing.

The Regulatory Action Policy confirms an assessment notice may be served in a number of circumstances where this course of action is *proportionate and appropriate*, including where:-

---

64 Page 8 of the policy

65 Section 146 DPA 2018

- a controller or processor has failed to respond to an information notice, or

- where there is a *probability personal data is not being processed in compliance with the data protection legislation, together with a likelihood of damage or distress to individuals,* and also

- where it is necessary to verify compliance with an enforcement notice.

In making a decision the Commissioner considers newspaper and other relevant reports such as reports from whistle blowers and data privacy impact assessments that may have been carried out.

Notices may be "urgent", "no-notice" or "short notice" depending on a number of factors, including the extent to which an investigation may prevent the risk of *serious harm to individuals or serious intrusion into their privacy.* Other considerations include the possible destruction, alteration or concealment of evidence, the scope of the notice, the burden on the recipient in having to comply with a notice on no-notice or short-notice, and the impact on the rights of the recipient if the Commissioner gains access without allowing them the opportunity to appeal. The comparative effectiveness of the Commissioner's other investigatory powers are also taken into account.

Section 146 (4) Data Protection Act 2018 provides: *An assessment notice must, in relation to each requirement imposed by the notice, specify the time or times at which, or period or periods within which, the requirement must be complied with.* The deadline for responding must not be shorter than the 28-day appeal deadline unless the notice is urgent in which case the deadline must not be less than seven days. [66]

---

[66] Section 146 (8) DPA 2018

In cases where the Commissioner considers there are reasonable grounds for suspecting that the controller or processor has failed to comply with section 149 (2) (this provision is set out in Chapter 2) or that an offence under the Data Protection Act 2018 has been committed, and it is necessary for the controller or processor to comply with a requirement in the notice in less than seven days, the notice may give a shorter deadline or compliance.. [67] The notice must identify the nature of the failure or offence and provide the reasons why a response is required within this shorter time frame.

Like information notices, assessment notices must provide information about the consequences of failing to comply and the rights of appeal. A notice may be cancelled by giving written notice to the recipients.

The Regulatory Action Policy confirms the Commissioner *may require access to the specified documents or information, or classes of documents or information, which define and explain how obligations have been met under the legislation, and the governance controls in place to measure compliance.* A non-exhaustive list of possible documents and information is given. It includes policies and procedures, training material, privacy statements, and privacy impact assessments.

Some of the material may be privileged or highly sensitive commercially. Individuals can contact the Commissioner to request that access to sensitive, privileged or other information be *limited to the minimum required to adequately assess their compliance with the legislation.* Such a request must be made within 28 days of the notice, unless the assessment is to be conducted on shorter notice, in which case the request should be made as soon as possible.

Inspections and examinations are described as key elements of the assessment. They may take place on site as part of a discussion with staff to demonstrate practice, or independently by way of sampling by

---

[67] Section 146 (9) ibid

auditors. Staff at all levels may be interviewed. Interviews are scheduled and agreed in advance of the on-site audit where possible. Should evidence of criminal activity emerge during an interview the interview will be halted. [68]

Data that is not specifically identified in the assessment notice may be taken off site only with the controller's permission.

Like information notices, where a recipient fails to respond to an assessment notice, the Commissioner will promptly apply to the court for an order requiring a response, depending on the reasons for non-compliance, any commitments given by the recipient, whether the information is likely to be available from another source, and the comparative effectiveness of other enforcement.[69]

The Commissioner will also consider whether to issue an enforcement notice as a result of the failure to comply.

Restrictions

There is a complete bar to allowing access to personal data processed for special purposes. Section 147 (5) simply provides; *The Commissioner may not give a controller or processor an assessment notice with respect to the processing of personal data for special purposes.* Unlike assessment notices, there is no provision allowing access where a special determination has been made.

The same restrictions covering privileged information apply as apply to information notices. The Regulatory Action Policy specifically confirms the Commissioner will require access to information which is subject to legal professional privilege and has a high level of commercial

68 Page 21 RAP

69 Pages 21 and 22 RAP

sensitivity.[70] All such privileged communications will be handled in accordance with the Attorney General's guidelines. [71]

There are no restrictions relating to evidence of criminal offences.

Criminal offences

Like information notices, under section 148 Data Protection Act 2018 it is an offence to destroy or falsify information and documents with the intention of preventing the Commissioner from viewing or being provided with the material. It is a defence to prove that the destruction, falsification etc would have occurred irrespective of the notice.

Publication

Assessment notices, urgent and no-notice assessment notices are likely to be published if:

- They are in the public domain;
- There is an expectation of an update or the ICO needs to show it has taken action
- Publication would help the assessment.[72]

At the time of writing they are not published on the page devoted to enforcement action on the ICO website.

---

70 Page 18 ibid

71 Page 22 ibid

72 Page ICO Communicating our Regulatory and Enforcement Activity Policy

Warrants for Forced Entry and Inspection (Dawn Raids)

The provisions relating to warrants are detailed and precise. Any failure to comply with them may undermine the lawfulness of the warrant and/or the lawfulness of the entry onto premises and the seizure of any documents. Such failures may give rise to civil claims for damages in trespass and trespass to goods and conversion.

Any warrant must allow the Commissioner to enter and search specified premises and *to inspect, examine, operate and test any equipment found on the premises which is used or intended to be used for the processing of personal data.* [73]

It must also authorise the Commissioner or any of his officers or staff to inspect and seize any material which is evidence of failures under section 149 (2) (see Chapter 2) or of an offence under the 2018 Act:[74] It must require a copy of information which may be evidence that is capable of being viewed using equipment on the premises. It must require any person on the premises to provide an explanation of any document, material or information and require any person to provide such other information as may reasonably be required to determine whether there has been a failure to comply with section 149 (2).

The actions authorised should be made clear on the warrant's face, with a deadline for executing the warrant seven days from issue. The judge issuing a warrant must also issue two certified copies.

A person executing a warrant issued under Schedule 15 may *use such reasonable force as may be necessary.* [75]

---

[73] Paragraph 5 (1) Schedule 15 DPA 2018

[74] Paragraph 5 ibid

[75] Paragraph 7, ibid8

Evidential conditions for issuing a warrant

Before issuing a warrant a judge must hear evidence on oath from the Commissioner and be satisfied of the following:-

1. There are reasonable grounds for suspecting that a controller or processor has or is failing to comply with section 149(2) Data Protection Act 2018 or that an offence under the Act has been committed, and there are also reasonable grounds for suspecting that evidence of the failure or offence is to be found on the premises or can be viewed using equipment on the premises; [76]

2. A controller or processor has failed to comply with a requirement imposed by an assessment notice, in which case the judge may issue a warrant relating to the premises specified in the assessment notice allowing the Commissioner to determine whether the controller or processor has or is complying with the data protection legislation. [77]

Procedural conditions for issuing a warrant

The following conditions must be met when issuing a warrant, unless compliance would defeat the object of entry to the premises or the Commissioner requires access to the premises urgently[78]:-

1. The Commissioner must have first given the occupier of the premises seven days' notice in writing demanding access (an

[76] Paragraph 1 (1) (b) ibid

[77] Paragraph 2 ibid

[78] Schedule 5 Paragraph 4 (1) ibid

assessment notice given to the occupier is to be disregarded for these purposes[79]) ;

2. Access to the premises must have been demanded at a reasonable hour and refused or, if entry to the premises was granted, the occupier unreasonably refused to comply with a request to be allowed to

    - search the premises;
    - inspect, examine, operate or test any equipment;
    - inspect and seize any documents or other material that might be evidence of a failure under section 149 (2) or of an offence;
    - require any person on the premises to provide a copy of information in an appropriate form *(so that it can be taken away and is visible and legible or can readily be made visible and legible)*[80] capable of being viewed using equipment on the premises;
    - require any person to provide an explanation of any document or other material found on the premises and any information capable of being viewed using equipment on the premises; and
    - *require any person on the premises to provide such other information as may reasonably be required for the purpose of*

---

[79] Paragraph 4 (5) ibid

[80] Schedule 15 paragraph 5 (5) DPA 2018

determining whether the controller or processor has failed or is failing as described in section 149 (2). [81]

3. Since any refusal, the occupier of the premises must have been notified of the application for a warrant and been given the opportunity to be heard by a judge on the question of whether or not the warrant should be issued.

Execution of warrant

A person executing a warrant may use such reasonable force as may be necessary. The warrant should be executed only at a reasonable hour unless the person exercising the warrant suspects doing so would defeat the object of the warrant.

If the occupier is present, the person executing the warrant must show them the warrant and give them a copy. Otherwise a copy of the warrant should be left in a prominent place on the premises.

Where anything is seized the person executing the warrant must, on request, give a receipt for it and give the occupier of the premises a copy of it, unless providing a copy would give rise to undue delay. *Anything seized may be retained for so long as is necessary in all the circumstances.* [82]

An executed warrant must be returned to the court from which it was issued endorsed with a statement from the person by whom it was executed describing the powers that were exercised under the warrant.

---

81 Paragraph 5, ibid

82 Paragraph 10 (4) ibid

Restrictions

There is no power to grant a warrant regarding personal data processed for special purposes unless a written determination under section 174 (see Chapter 2) has taken effect.

The powers granted by a warrant may not be exercised regarding privileged material concerning the data protection legislation This exemption does not apply to anything held by third parties (ie by parties other than the legal adviser and client) or anything held with the intention of furthering a criminal purpose.

Offences

It is an offence to obstruct a person executing a warrant, or to fail to give that person such assistance as they may reasonably require without reasonable excuse, or to make a false statement in response to a query during a visit under warrant.[83]

Civil claims

Failures to comply with the provisions of Schedule 5 Data Protection Act 2018 may give rise to a civil claim for damages in trespass, trespass to goods and conversion.

83 Paragraph 15 Schedule 15 DPA 2018

CHAPTER SIX

COMMISSIONER'S CORRECTIVE POWERS: ENFORCEMENT NOTICES

Introduction

After investigating how data processing operations are carried out, the Commissioner may decide to exercise his corrective powers by issuing enforcement and penalty notices under Article 58 UK GDPR. [84]

Article 58 (2) gives him extensive corrective powers which include:-

- Issuing warnings to a controller or processor that their intended processing operations are likely to infringe provisions of the Regulation;

- Issuing reprimands where processing operations have already infringed provisions of the Regulation;

- Ordering the controller or processor to comply with the data subject's requests to exercise their rights under the Regulation, such as their right of access to their personal data;

- Ordering the controller or processor to bring their processing operations into compliance with the provisions of the Regulation *in a specified manner and within a specified time*;

[84] See also section 149 Data Protection Act 2018

- Ordering the controller to communicate a personal data breach to the data subject;

- Imposing a *temporary or definitive limitation including a ban on processing;*

- Ordering the rectification or erasure of personal data or restriction of processing and the notification of such actions to persons to whom the personal data have been disclosed;

- Imposing an administrative fine pursuant to Article 83 UK GDPR in addition to or instead of other corrective measures *depending on the circumstances of each individual case*;

- Ordering *the suspensions of data flows to a recipient in a third country or to an international organisation.*

Warnings, reprimands and administrative fines are not covered by enforcement notices.

Enforcement notices

An enforcement notice requires an undertaking to take the steps specified in the notice or to refrain from taking those steps by a specified time. Failure to comply with the notice may result in a penalty notice (fine).

The Commissioner's Regulatory Action Policy confirms:

> *The purpose of an enforcement notice is to mandate action (or halt action, such as processing or transfer) to bring about compliance with information rights and/or remedy a breach. Failure to comply with an enforcement notice invites further action, including the possibility of the ICO issuing a civil monetary penalty.*

Such a notice may be issued *inter alia* where the Commissioner is satisfied that a person has failed as described under section 149 (2) ie failed to[85]:

- Comply with the data protection principles;
- Allow a data subject to exercise their rights;
- Comply with their obligations as a data controller or processor;
- Communicate a personal data breach to the Commissioner or a data subject;
- Comply with the principles for transfers of personal data to third countries.

In deciding whether to issue a notice for such a failure *the Commissioner must consider whether the failure has caused or is likely to cause any person damage or distress.*[86] Reference is made to this requirement in the notices sent to Smith Law and Shepherd IFA Ltd and to First Choice Selection Services in the cases outlined, below. Although the Commissioner considered damage and distress was unlikely, he decided an enforcement notice was appropriate for Smith Law and Shepherd.

His powers in relation to section 149 (2) failures extend to imposing a ban on all processing or imposing a ban on some data processing by reference to:-

- A description of personal data;
- The purpose or manner of processing;

---

85 Section 149 (1) and (2) DPA 2018

86 Section 150 (2) ibid

- The time when the processing takes place.

However, notices to remedy section 149 (2) failings are not punitive. They may only impose requirements which the Commissioner considers appropriate for remedying the failures. [87]

A penalty notice may be issued against a controller at the same time as an enforcement notice in many circumstances including , for example, where an undertaking has failed to pay the data controller registration fee to the ICO.

Contents of an enforcement notice

Any enforcement notice requires close scrutiny so as to check for compliance with the statutory requirements. Otherwise, there may be grounds for appeal.

It must state what the person has failed or is failing to do and give reasons for the Commissioner reaching this decision.[88] It must provide information about the consequences of failing to comply with the notice and the rights of appeal.[89] Any deadline for compliance must not fall before the deadline for making any appeal[90], which is 28 days from receipt of the notice

Where an appeal is made, the requirements of the notice are suspended pending its outcome or the withdrawal of the appeal.[91]

---

87 Section 149 (6) ibid

88 Section 150 (1) ibid

89 Section 150 (5) ibid

90 Section 150 (7) ibid

91 Section 150 (6) ibid

Urgent enforcement notices

There are cases where deadlines for compliance with any notice need to be shorter than 28 days. In these circumstances an urgent enforcement notice is sent. The Commissioner must give his reasons for deciding the notice is urgent in the notice. Any deadlines for compliance may not be earlier than 24 hours from the giving of the notice but they may be earlier than the deadline for lodging an appeal. [92]

Deciding that an enforcement notice is urgent is a significant step. When making this decision and setting the deadline for compliance, the Commissioner must consider whether urgent action is *appropriate and proportionate* taking into account:

- whether such action may prevent or limit the risk of serious harm to individuals or serious intrusion into their privacy;
- the scope of the enforcement notice;
- the burden on the recipient in having to comply in the short period specified; and
- the comparative effectiveness of other enforcement powers.[93]

Enforcement notice for rectification and erasure of personal data and expressions of opinion

An enforcement notice may require a controller or processor to rectify or erase inaccurate personal data as a result of a failure to comply with the

[92] Section 150 (8) DPA 2018

[93] Page 23RAP.

data protection principal of accuracy[94], or allow a data subject to exercise their rights to rectify, erase or restrict the processing of their personal data;

Such a notice may also require the rectification or erasure of other data that *contains an expression of opinion that appears to the Commissioner to be based on the inaccurate personal data.* [95] The notice may also require notification of the rectification or erasure to third parties to whom the data has been disclosed.

Rather more convoluted provisions deal with data that has been accurately recorded by the controller but is said to be inaccurate. In these circumstances the enforcement notice may require the controller or processor to take specified steps (depending on the purpose of the processing) to ensure the data is accurate or, *secure that the data indicates the data subject's view that the data is inaccurate and to supplement the data with a statement of the true facts relating to the matters dealt with by the data that is approved by the Commissioner.* [96]

Cancellation and variation

Where there has been a change in circumstances which means that one or more of the provisions in the enforcement notice need not be complied with in order to remedy the failure, the recipient may apply to the Commissioner in writing for the notice to be cancelled or varied. [97]

---

[94] As provided in Article 5 (1) (d) UK GDPR or section 38(1) or section 89 DPA 2018 (see section 151 (8))

[95] Section 151 (2) DPA 2018

[96] Section 151 (3) (c) DPA 2018

[97] Section 153 (2) ibid

Such an application may be made only where the deadline for making an appeal has passed.

Restrictions

Processing for special purposes has a judicial safeguard before enforcement notices or penalty notices may be sent that cover personal data processed for these purposes.

There is no power to give an enforcement notice in relation to data processed for special purposes unless the Commissioner has made a determination under section 174 (see Chapter 2) *and* a court has granted leave for the notice to be given.

The court must not grant leave unless satisfied the Commissioner *has reason to suspect a failure described in section 149 (2) which is of substantial public importance*[98], and the controller or processor has either been given notice of the application for leave or the case is urgent.

There are also restrictions in relation to parliamentary privilege and the processing of personal data by a joint controller.

Publication

The ICO's Communicating Our Regulatory and Enforcement Activity Policy confirms it will publish enforcement notices if it will help promote good practice or deter non-compliance. The same applies to warnings and reprimands. All can be viewed on the ICO's website by industry sector.

---

[98] Section 152 (2) ibid

Enforcement notices on the website at the time of writing almost all concern breaches of PECR: mainly unsolicited marketing calls and texts.

Recent examples

Recent examples of enforcement notices that do not concern breaches of PECR focus on failure or delay in responding to data subject access requests. They tend to be issued when a controller repeatedly ignores subject access requests and interventions on behalf of the Commissioner.

Smith Law and Shepherd IFA Limited – 14 February 2022

Smith Law and Shepherd IFA Limited (SLS) offers independent advice on investments, pensions and mortgages and is a data controller. Two individuals, data subjects 1 and 2, made access requests for their personal data which were repeatedly ignored. When they complained to the Information Commissioner, his case worker wrote to SLS at least twice, requiring it to respond to the subject access request in seven days. SLS ignored the Commissioner also. When the case worker telephoned SLS he was told that the request had been satisfied by sending information to the Financial Ombudsman's Service. The case worker wrote to SLS again, instructing it to respond in seven days and making it clear that providing information to the Financial Ombudsman's Service was not sufficient to satisfy its obligations under the data protection legislation. SLS continued to ignore the data subject access requests.

The Commissioner decided SLS had contravened Article 15 of the GDPR in failing to inform the data subjects, without undue delay, whether their personal data was being processed and, if that was the case, in failing to provide access to such personal data, again without undue delay. The case worker sent SLS an enforcement notice requiring them to comply with the data subject access requests within a month. Given the delay of nearly two years since the access requests had been submitted in April 2020, this was *a necessary and proportionate regulatory step.*

When deciding to send an enforcement notice the Commissioner considered, as he was required to do under section 150 (4) Data Protection Act 2018, whether the contravention had caused, or was likely to cause, damage or distress to the data subject. Although no damage or distress had been caused in this case he decided an enforcement notice was a necessary and proportionate step to bring SLS into compliance. The contravention was significant, particularly given the length of time that had elapsed since the subject access requests had been submitted almost two years previously.

<u>First Choice Selection Services Ltd</u> – 2 March 2021

This is an interesting notice which confirms that ongoing proceedings do not justify refusing to comply with a data subject access request.

First Choice Selection Services Ltd (FCSS) is a recruitment agency and data controller. It received a data subject access request from one of its employees, who had issued proceedings against it in the Employment Tribunal. It replied by asserting that the data subject had a right to information that was relevant to their claim and not to anything else.

The data subject complained to the Commissioner in May 2020. The Commissioner's case worker wrote to the controller the following month, reminding it of its obligations under the data protection legislation and requiring it to take appropriate steps to respond to the request. There was no reply. The case worker telephoned and wrote again twice, on the last occasion requiring the controller to reply in seven days with an appropriate response or with a time scale for responding. When FCSS failed to comply the case worker sent a further letter concluding that the controller had infringed data protection legislation. In reply, FCSS confirmed the data subject was involved in ongoing Employment Tribunal proceedings against the controller and that:

In discussions with the Judge around the issues of documents we were instructed to release no information at this stage and as part of the ongoing case we will be instructed to release appropriate documents to [the Data Subject] as required for the case.

When it failed to produce any evidence to support this contention, and the data subject produced an email from the Tribunal which confirmed that it had no jurisdiction to deal with matters relating to data protection requests the Commissioner sent the Controller an enforcement notice. The controller was required to respond to the data subject access request and to

- change its internal systems, procedures and policies to ensure that future subject access requests were identified and complied with *subject only to the proper application of any exemption from, or restriction or adaptation of, the right of subject access provided for in or by virtue of the UK GDPR or DPA.*

Appeals

An undertaking that receives an enforcement notice may appeal against the notice and against any one or more urgency statements in the notice to the First-tier Tribunal (General Regulatory Chamber.) An appeal also lies against deadlines in any urgency notice. [99]

It may also appeal against the Commissioner's refusal of an application to vary or cancel an enforcement notice[100] on account of a change in circumstances.

[99] Section 162 and 164 DPA 2018

[100] Section 162 (1) and (2) ibid

An appeal against an enforcement notice may ask the Tribunal to review the findings of fact the Commissioner made when deciding to issue the notice. [101]

It may also rely on the notice's failure to comply with the law, or argue that any discretion the Commissioner exercised should have been exercised differently.[102] If the Tribunal agrees the notice is unlawful or the Commissioner should have exercised his discretion differently the Tribunal must allow the appeal . Alternatively it may substitute the notice with another notice the Commissioner could have given. Otherwise it must dismiss the appeal.

The procedure for applications to the First-tier and Upper-tier Tribunals is considered in Chapter 8.

---

[101] Section 163 (2) ibid

[102] Section 163 ibid

CHAPTER SEVEN

COMMISSIONER'S CORRECTIVE POWERS: PENALTY NOTICES

Introduction

Among the headline grabbing changes introduced by the GDPR was the increase in fines. A penalty notice, which is a written notice requiring a person to pay the Commissioner an amount, is the mechanism for imposing a fine.

The power to issue such a notice arises in a number of circumstances, including those where a person has failed as described in section 149 (2) (see Chapter 2), or has failed to comply with an information notice, an assessment notice or an enforcement notice.[103] In this respect penalty notices may be described as a measure of last resort. The Commissioner's Regulatory Action Policy refers to the system of enforcement as a *hierarchy of regulatory action.*

A fine may be imposed in addition to or instead of the other corrective measures listed at the beginning of the previous chapter. [104] For example, the ICO website publishes a number of enforcement notices which have been issued in tandem with penalty notices.

As ever, it is of the utmost importance to engage closely and effectively with the Commissioner in the aftermath of any breach. The case summaries at the end of this chapter outline the Commissioner's approach when investigating a breach and considering the penalty.

---

[103] Section 155 (1) DPA 2018

[104] Article 83 (2) UK GDPR

Factors considered

When deciding whether to give a penalty notice, and then when going on to decide the amount, the Commissioner must ensure that the fine is *effective, proportionate and dissuasive* [105] and also have regard to the considerations listed in Article 83 (2) UK GDPR. Given their importance, these are set out in full below:

(a) *the nature, gravity and duration of the infringement taking into account the nature, scope or purpose of the processing concerned as well as the number of data subjects affected and the level of damage suffered by them;*

(b) *the intentional or negligent character of the infringement;*

(c) *any action taken by the controller or processor to mitigate the damage suffered by data subjects;*

(d) *the degree of responsibility of the controller or processor taking into account technical and organisational measures implemented by them….;*

(e) *any relevant previous infringements by the controller or processor;*

(f) *the degree of co-operation with the Commissioner in order to remedy the infringement and mitigate the possible adverse effects of the infringement;*

(g) *the categories of personal data affected by the infringement;*

(h) *the manner in which the infringement became known to the Commissioner, in particular whether, and if so to what*

[105] Article 83 (1) ibid

extent, the controller or processor notified of the infringement;

(i) *where measures referred to in Article 58 (2) have previously been ordered against the controller or processor concerned with regard to the same subject matter, compliance with those measures;*

(j) *adherence to approved codes of conduct….. and*

(k) *any other aggravating or mitigating factor applicable to the circumstances of the case such as financial benefit gained or losses avoided, directly or indirectly from the infringement.*

RAP reflects these requirements and confirms that penalty notices are reserved for the most serious cases, typically involving *wilful, deliberate or negligent acts, or repeated breaches of information rights obligations, causing harm or damage to individuals. In considering the degree of harm or damage we may consider that, where there is a lower level of impact across a large number of individuals, that the totality of that damage or harm may be substantial, and may require a sanction.* [106]

Hence a penalty notice is more likely where: special category data are involved; *there has been a repeated breach of obligations or a failure to rectify a previously identified problem or follow previous recommendations; wilful action (including inaction) is a feature of the case* ; there has been a failure to apply reasonable measures such as privacy by design to mitigate any breach (or the possibility of it); there has been a failure to implement the accountability provision of the GDPR.

[106] Page 25 RAP

Representations

Before issuing a penalty notice the Commissioner must advise, what he calls *the target,* by sending them a notice of intent. [107]The notice sets out the circumstances of the breach, the findings of the Commissioner's investigation and the proposed level of penalty. A rationale for the penalty is provided, together with any enforcement notice requirements.

The target is given a maximum of 21 days from receipt of the notice to make written representations in response. No penalty notice may be provided before this deadline has passed. [108] Furthermore, the Commissioner may not give a penalty notice in reliance on a notice of intent after a period of six months from the date when the notice of intent is given has expired. [109] The period may be extended by agreement between the Commissioner and the target.

In cases the Commissioner considers exceptional, the target may be permitted to make oral face to face representations in the Commissioner's office. RAP confirms that such a meeting may be appropriate where:

- the central facts of a breach or failing are in dispute;
- *the integrity of any technical witness evidence is in dispute;*
- there is a requirement to make reasonable adjustments under the Equality Act 2010; or
- *the consideration of "harm" elements of a case would benefit from evidence from those affected.*[110]

---

[107] Paragraph 2 (1) Schedule 16 DPA 2018

[108] Paragraph 4 (1) ibid

[109] Paragraph 2 (2) and (3) ibid

[110] Page 5 RAP

The policy is clear that the Commissioner is unlikely to agree to oral representations in a case that is principally technical in nature. Complex technical cases are better considered in writing.

Contents of a penalty notice

Penalty notices are lengthy documents. Under paragraph 5, Schedule 16 of the Data Protection Act 2018, a notice must contain the following information:-

- the name and address of the person to whom it is addressed;
- details of the notice of intent given to the person;
- whether the Commissioner received oral or written representations;
- the reasons why the Commissioner is imposing the penalty, including a description of the circumstances of the failure and, where the failing comes within section 149 (2) (see Chapter 2) , the nature of the personal data involved in the failure;
- the reasons for the amount of the penalty, including any aggravating or mitigating factors that the Commissioner has taken into account;
- details of how the penalty is to be paid and the period within which it is to be paid (which must be not less than 28 days from the date when the penalty notice is given [111]);
- details of the rights of appeal;

[111] Paragraph 6 (2) Schedule 16 DPA 2018

- details of the Commissioner's enforcement powers.

Variation and cancellation of a penalty notice

The Commissioner may vary a penalty notice by giving written notice. A penalty variation notice may not reduce the period for payment of the penalty, increase the amount of the penalty or *otherwise vary the penalty notice to the detriment of the person to whom it was given.* [112]

A penalty notice may also be cancelled by the Commissioner on written notice. Once that has been given he may not take any further action in relation to the failure that was the subject of the notice, and must repay any fine.[113] In other words the Commissioner may not reopen the case once he has cancelled it.

Enforcement

No action may be taken to recover a fine until the deadline for paying it has passed, the 28-day deadline for appealing has expired, and any appeals have been decided, including any appeal against a variation in the notice.[114]

In England and Wales a penalty is recoverable upon application to either the county court or High Court.

[112] Paragraph 7 (3) ibid

[113] Paragraph 8 (2) ibid

[114] See generally Paragraph 9 Schedule 16 DPA 2018

Restrictions

The same restrictions apply to penalty notices given for failings within the meaning of section 149 (2) as apply to enforcement notices (see preceding chapter). [115]

Penalty Amount

The maximum fine for an undertaking is £17,500,000 or up to 4% of an undertaking's total worldwide annual turnover in the preceding financial year, whichever is the higher. This is known as "the higher maximum amount". [116] Such a fine may be given in relation to breaches of the principles of data processing, breaches of the data subject's rights and breaches relating to international transfers, together with failures to comply with an information notice, an assessment notice or an enforcement notice.[117]

The "standard maximum amount" for an undertaking is £8,700,000 or 2% of the undertaking's total annual worldwide turnover in the preceding financial year, whichever is the higher.[118] This level of fine applies to breaches of: Article 32 concerning the security of data processing (see the Marriott and British Airways fines below); the notification provisions for data breaches; the requirement to carry out of data impact assessments; the requirement to designate a data protection officer and other largely administrative breaches.

RAP sets out the following mechanism for deciding the amount of any penalty:

---

[115] Section 156 DPA 2018

[116] Section 157 (5) DPA 2018

[117] Article 83 (5) UK GDPR and section 157 (1) UK GDPR

[118] Article 83 (4) and Section 157 (6) DPA 2018

- **Step 1**: An "initial element" removing any financial gain from the breach;

- **Step 2**: Adding in an element to censure the breach based on its scale and severity, taking into account the matters listed under *Factors Considered* above;

- **Step 3**: Adding in an element to reflect any aggravating factors;

- **Step 4:** Adding in an amount for deterrent effect to others;

- **Step 5:** Reducing the amount (save the initial element) to reflect any mitigating factors, including the ability to pay (financial hardship).

The amount will be higher where:-

- *vulnerable individuals or critical national infrastructure have been affected;*

- *there has been deliberate action for financial or personal gain;*

- *advice, guidance, recommendations or warnings (including those from a Data Protection Officer or the ICO) have been ignored or not acted upon;*

- *there has been a high degree of intrusion into the privacy of a data subject;*

- *there has been a failure to co-operate with an ICO investigation or enforcement notice; and*

- *there is a pattern of poor regulatory history by the target of the investigation.*[119]

If a controller or processor infringes several provisions of the UK GDPR for the same or linked processing operations, the total amount of the fine will not exceed the amount specified for the most serious infringement.[120] In other words fines cannot be aggregated for different breaches of the data protection legislation in these circumstances.

The Commissioner collects the fines and pays them to HM Treasury and the Consolidated Fund.

Appeals

There is a right of appeal to the First-tier Tribunal (General Regulatory Chamber) (the Tribunal) against a penalty notice and/or its amount. [121]

When deciding an appeal the Tribunal may review any determination of facts on which the notice was based. If the Tribunal considers that any discretion exercised by the Commissioner should have been exercised differently, it must allow the appeal or substitute another notice which the Commissioner could have given.[122] An appeal will also be allowed and another notice may be substituted where the technical requirements for the notice itself have been infringed.

Chapter 8 considers the procedure for appeals to the First-tier and Upper-tier Tribunals.

---

[119] Page 27 ICO Regulatory Action Policy

[120] Article 83 (3) UK GDPR

[121] Section 162 (3) DPA 2018

[122] Section 163 (3) ibid

Recent examples

Marriott International Inc – 30 October 2020

In October 2020 the ICO used its new powers under the GDPR to impose significantly increased fines for the first time in two cases. One of the two involved Marriott International Inc, an international hotel chain with its operational headquarters in the USA. It had acquired Starwood Hotels and Resorts Worldwide Inc ("Starwood") in 2016.

By the time Marriott had acquired Starwood, an unknown attacker had been gaining access to Starwood's computer systems for two years. Starwood knew nothing of this and neither did Marriott. After the acquisition Marriott made enhancements to Starwood's network and the Starwood system continued to operate separately from Marriott's, although it planned to integrate *aspects of the Starwood network in the Marriott network over an 18- month period in order to create a single unified network within Marriott's security network.*[123]

The attacker continued to traverse through the Starwood system gaining access to customers' payment card data. The attack was not discovered until September 2018 when the attacker counted the rows in a table containing cardholder information, which triggered an alert. Marriott instigated its Information and Privacy Incident Response Plan two or three days later.

The attacker obtained personal data that was both encrypted and unencrypted. The unencrypted personal data included:-

- guest name, gender, date of birth, whether the guest had been identified as a VIP, whether they were a member of the Starwood loyalty programme and their account information, mailing address, passport country code, 5.2. million unencrypted guest passport numbers (of which 935,000 were associated with EEA

[123] Paragraph 3.4 Penalty Notice.

member state records) phone number, fax number, email address and credit card expiration date.

The encrypted personal data included:-

- 18.5 million passport numbers, 4,290,00 of which were associated with EEA member state records, and 9.1 million encrypted payment cards, 870,000 of which were associated with EEA member state records.

Some of the personal data affected belonged to data subjects based in various countries within the European Union, and the Information Commissioner acted as lead supervisory authority when imposing a fine.

On 22 November 2018 Marriott notified the Commissioner of a personal data breach. On 30 November 2018 Marriott provided a follow-up report to the Commissioner regarding further personal data breaches, issued a press release about the attack and established a dedicated Starwood incident website, and also sent an email notification to data subjects informing them that a call centre had been set up to receive complaints.

On 5 July 2019 the Commissioner notified Marriott of her intention to impose a penalty of £99,200,396. Marriott made extensive and complex written representations in reply in August 2019. After the Commissioner had provided Marriott with a draft decision in December 2019 and an extension of the six-month time limit for issuing a penalty notice had been agreed, Marriott provided a second set of representations in January 2022 when it submitted further relevant evidence. Marriott does not appear to have requested an opportunity to make oral submissions. Eventually two further extensions were agreed for issuing the penalty notice. The last agreed deadline was 30 September 2020.

The Commissioner proposed further submissions and an extension due to the complexity of the case, Marriott's representations and the fact that this was one of the first major decisions under the new EU data protection regime.

She determined that Marriott had failed adequately to prepare the Starwood information technology systems to protect personal data, when the GDPR came into effect on 25 May 2018. The target had failed to comply with its security obligations under Article 5 (1) (f) and Article 32 of the GDPR.

The Commissioner concluded that there were four principal failures in security:-

1. Insufficient monitoring of privileged user accounts so that the attacker's access to these accounts was undetected. The Commissioner referred to guidance from the National Cyber Security Centre that had recommended monitoring as one of ten steps an organisation could take to protect themselves in cyberspace;

2. Insufficient monitoring of data bases, including the failure to log actions such as the creation of files and the exporting of entire data base tables by the attacker;

3. The absence of control of critical systems, including the failure to implement a form of server hardening as a preventative measure *which could have prevented the attacker from gaining access to administrator accounts and performing reconnaissance before traversing across a network.*

4. The absence of encryption. It should have been applied to other categories of personal data, in addition to passport and card details.

When reaching her decision to impose a penalty notice, the Commissioner responded in detail to Marriott's representations. Her replies included the following observations:-

- *Not every instance of unauthorised processing or breach of security will necessarily amount to a breach of Article 5 or Article 32. The obligation under Article 5 GDPR is to ensure "appropriate" security; the obligation under Article 32 is to implement "appropriate" technical and organisational measures to ensure an "appropriate" level of security, taking account of the state of the art, the costs of implementation and the nature, scope, context and purposes of processing, as well as the risk to the rights of data subjects.*[124]

- When considering whether there has been a breach of the GDPR and whether to impose a penalty, she had to avoid reasoning purely with the benefit of hindsight.[125]

- Her findings did not involve applying the benefit of hindsight. There were four distinct weaknesses in Marriott's system, each of which it ought to have identified and rectified using one of the range of options available.

- She did not rely on:

  the "success" of the attack as evidence that a breach of the GDPR definitely occurred. Instead, the attacker's ability to exploit deficiencies in Marriott's security measures, for which remedies were available, discloses wider failures to put appropriate measures in place... The measures... could have been implemented using standard industry tools, and could have prevented, detected and/or mitigated the impact of the Attack. What the Attack disclosed was the failure by Marriott to put in place appropriate security measures to

[124] Paragraph 6.5 Penalty Notice

[125] Paragraph 6.6 ibid

> *address attacks of this kind and/or other identifiable risks to the system.* [126]

- She made it clear that:

> *the fact an IT systems is due to be retired shortly does not disapply the GDPR to the data being processed through that system. Marriott was still obliged to decide what appropriate measures should be in place in the light of the continued use of the system. While the fact that a system is to be decommissioned may be a relevant factor in determining what measures would be appropriate in a given case, this ultimately does not remove the basic obligation to put in place security measures appropriate to the risk of the continued processing.*[127]

- A breach of the security principal of data processing under Article 5 (f) attracts the higher amount of maximum fine. Although a breach of Article 32 attracts the standard maximum amount the breach of article 5 means the Commissioner may impose the higher maximum amount because that is the graver breach.[128]

After taking into account mitigating factors, including the impact of the Covid-19 pandemic, the fine was assessed at £18.4 million. In reaching this figure the Commissioner used the five steps described in her Regulatory Action Policy:-

Step 1: No adjustment as Marriott did not gain any financial benefit or avoid any losses as a result of its security breach.

---

[126] Paragraph 6.55 ibid

[127] Paragraph 6.59 ibid

[128] Paragraph 7.56 ibid

Step 2:

The nature, gravity and duration of the failures:

> *...there were multiple measures that Marriott could have put in place that would have allowed for the detection of or mitigated the attack in so far as it continued after 25 May 2018. What the attack shows is that during the relevant period Marriott was processing data on a system that had multiple security failings that were exploited by the attacker and could have been exploited by others.*[129]

An extremely large number of individuals had been affected by the breach. Although the mitigating steps taken by Marriott might have mitigated their distress, it was nevertheless likely that some of the affected individuals had still suffered anxiety and distress as a result of the disclosure of their personal information (including payment card information) to an unknown individual or individuals. The fact that Marriott received 57,000 calls relating to the breach was indicative of the potential concern among data subjects. *Marriott's suggestion that distress will only arise in cases where they are advised by their banks to cancel their payment cards ignores the fact that all personal data (not just financial data) is of significance to individuals, a significance which is reflected in the legal protections afforded to that data under the GDPR.*[130]

There was no evidence of financial damage suffered by any individual and this was not taken into account when setting the fine.

---

[129] Paragraph 7.9 ibid

[130] Paragraph 7.12 (e) of the penalty notice

The infringements occurred over a period of nearly four months and this was a *significant period of time over which unauthorised access to personal data went undetected and/or unremedied.* [131]

The intentional or negligent character of the infringement:

The Commissioner recognised that the infringement had not been intentional or deliberate. However, she did consider that Marriott had been negligent in maintaining systems that suffered from vulnerabilities and short comings. She said: *a company of the size and profile of Marriott is expected to be aware that it is likely to be targeted by attackers, sophisticated or otherwise. Marriott must be aware that the nature of its business involves processing large volumes of personal data, including sensitive personal data. The risk of any compromise of that information may have significant consequences for Marriott's customers and its own business.* [132]

Any action taken by the controller or processor to mitigate the damages suffered by data subjects:

The Commissioner decided to consider this issue separately under Step 5.

The degree of responsibility of the controller or processor:

The Commissioner considered Marriott was wholly responsible for the breaches. The engagement of third parties to implement, manage or maintain certain elements of the system did not reduce Marriott's responsibility for the identified breaches. *In circumstances where Marriott accepts that it is the relevant data controller, and significant failures in its*

---

[131] Paragraph 7.13 ibid

[132] Paragraph 7.17 ibid

security measures have been identified, the engagement of third parties cannot reduce its degree of responsibility. [133]

The fact that Marriott may have complied with certain industry guidance focusing on specific types of personal data did not obviate or reduce its responsibility for the security of all the personal data it held.

Relevant previous infringements:

The absence of any previous infringements was taken into account when deciding to impose and penalty and also when setting its amount.

Degree of cooperation with the supervisory authority:

Marriott had co-operated fully with her investigation.

Categories of personal data affected:

See above.

Manner in which the infringement became known to the Commissioner:

The Commissioner accepted that Marriott had complied with its obligations to notify her.

Taking into account the need to provide an *affective, proportionate and dissuasive* fine for a controller of Marriott's scale and turnover, the Commissioner considered that a penalty of £28 million was appropriate,

[133] Paragraph 7.28 ibid

before adjustment in accordance with Steps 3-5 below and the application of the Commissioner's Covid -19 policy.

Step 3: The Commissioner did not consider there were any aggravating factors.

Following the alert Marriott promptly informed affected data subjects and took immediate steps to mitigate the effects of the attack and implement remedial measures.

Step 4: The Commissioner considered the penalty was already large enough to be dissuasive. She was unaware of any widespread issues of poor practice which might be deterred by the imposition of a higher penalty.

Step 5: The Commissioner took into account a number of factors when reducing the fine by 20% from £28 million to £22.4 million:

- The increase in the size of Marriott's budget for IT security following the breach;

- The immediate steps Marriott had taken to mitigate the effect of the attack and protect the interests of data subjects (but not the financial cost of those steps, which was not directly relevant to the amount of the penalty);

- Marriott's full cooperation with her investigation;

- The widespread reporting in the media which was likely to have increased the awareness of other data controllers of the risks posed by cyber-attacks and of the need to ensure they took all appropriate measures to secure personal data;

- The adverse effect of the attack and subsequent regulatory action on the Marriott brand and reputation which was likely to have a dissuasive effect on Marriott and other data controllers;

Although the Commissioner considered the level of fine would not cause financial hardship to Marriott, it was appropriate to reduce the penalty by a further £2 million *in light of the current public health emergency and associated economic consequences.* [134]

British Airways – 16 October 2018

British Airways (BA) was the other initial target for a fine under the new GDPR. Between 22 June and 5 September 2018 it was the victim of a cyber-attack. During this period card holder data was extracted from the BritishAirways.com website to an external third-party domain controlled by the attacker. The attacker had gained access to this and other information through a remote access gateway used by a third-party provider to BA, and so this was described as a breach of supply chain security.

The personal data involved belonged to about 430,000 individuals and included names, addresses, card and CVV numbers in some instances. There was the possibility of identity theft from some individuals, although the attacker appeared to be motivated purely by financial gain and achieving access to the payment cards.

On 6 September 2018 BA notified the Commissioner of the attack. The Commissioner commenced an investigation and issued BA with a Notice of Intent on 4 July 2019. The proposed penalty was £183.39 million. BA then submitted written representations and provided further information in its response. There was toing and froing with requests from and provision of additional information to the Commissioner. She agreed to give BA the opportunity to make further representations if it agreed to extending the six-month period for issuing a penalty notice. The statutory deadline for issuing the penalty notice was eventually extended

[134] Para 7.53 penalty notice

to 30 September 2020 by agreement. In the meantime, BA made oral submissions by video call on 2 July 2020.

When deciding to provide a penalty notice and assessing the level of penalty, the Commissioner took into account the following considerations:

Step 1: No financial gain or reduction of loss

Step 2:

Nature and gravity of failure

- It was unclear whether BA would have detected the breach in the absence of an alert from a third party;
- A significant number of data subjects were affected;
- Notwithstanding all the assurances and mitigating steps taken by BA, individuals were likely to have suffered anxiety and distress. The Commissioner referred to 40,000 data subjects taking up BA's offer of free credit monitoring.

Duration

- The infringement had lasted from 25 May 2018 (when the GDPR came into force) to 5 September 2018. *This was a significant period of time (103 days) during which unauthorised access to, and in some cases subsequent exfiltration of, personal data went undetected by BA.*

The intentional or negligent character of the infringement

- The breach was not an intentional or deliberate act by BA. However, BA was negligent;

- Deficiencies in BA's system had been present for some time. The advent of the GDPR should have prompted a careful review of their systems and security.

The degree of responsibility of the controller or processor

- *There were numerous deficiencies in BA's security measures and network which the attack exposed;*

- *The attacker was able to exploit the deficiencies in BA's security, ultimately gaining access to personal data that should not have been accessible using the third-party remote access system.*

Any relevant previous infringements or any previous failure to comply with any enforcement or penalty notices

- None

Degree of co-operation with the Commissioner

- Full co-operation.

Manner in which infringement became known to the Commissioner

BA acted promptly in notifying the Commissioner

After taking into account the need to apply an *effective, proportionate and dissuasive fine in the context of a controller of BA's scale and turnover* the Commissioner determined a penalty of £30 million would be appropriate, before adjustment to reflect steps 3-5 below and the application of the Commissioner's Covid 19 policy.

<u>Step 3:</u> There were no aggravating factors.

<u>Step 4</u>: There was no need to increase the fine to dissuade others.

<u>Step 5</u>: Mitigating factors

- BA took immediate measures to mitigate and minimise any damage suffered by data subjects. (As with the Marriott case, it was not appropriate to reduce the penalty to reflect costs incurred by BA in taking measures to rectify or mitigate the impact of its infringement, including the cost of appointing external forensic consultants or legal advisers.)

- BA promptly informed affected data subjects, other law enforcement and regulatory agencies and the Commissioner, and fully co-operated with the Commissioner's enquiry thereafter.

- Widespread reporting in the media was likely to have increased the awareness of other data controllers of risks posed by cyber-attacks and the need to take appropriate security measures.

- The attack and subsequent regulatory action had adversely affected BA's brand and reputation which would have had some dissuasive effect on BA and other data controllers

The fine was reduced by 20%, to £24 million after taking into account mitigating factors. It was then further reduced to £20 million to reflect the financial impact of Covid.

Clearview AI Inc – 18 May 2022

Clearview AI Inc (Clearview) is an undertaking which operates an algorithmic search engine. *It provides a service whereby a customer can seek to match an image that is of interest to the customer (a "Probe Image") against a data base of images, metadata and URLs held by Clearview.* Clearview derives a set of facial vectors (biometric data) from the Probe Image which it compares to facial vectors drawn from images on its data base. Clearview then provides the customer with search results which show images that have similar characteristics.

Clearview obtains the images from the internet world wide (including from social media websites). There are images of a very substantial number of UK residents held on its data base . It takes no steps to exclude UK residents, although under Article 3 UK GDPR the Regulation applies to the processing of personal data of data subjects who are in the United Kingdom by a controller or processor not established in the UK where the processing activities are related to *the monitoring of their behaviour as far as their behaviour takes place within the United Kingdom.*[135] Clearview accepted that if the UK GDPR were applicable, which it denied, any contention that it had complied with its provisions was hopeless.

The Commissioner determined there were extensive breaches, including breaches of the principles of lawfulness, fairness and transparency and of the principle of storage limitation under Article 5 (a) and (e) respectively. There was no lawful basis for the processing under Article 6 or under Article 9, which concerns special category data (in this case biometric data). Furthermore, data subjects had not been allowed to exercise their rights of access, their right to rectification and erasure, their right to object to processing and their right not to be subject to decisions based solely on automated decision-making including profiling. There had also

[135] Article 3 (2) (b)

been a beach of the duty to carry out a Data Protection Impact Assessment under Article 35 UK GDPR.

A penalty notice was issued for £7,552,800. The Commissioner noted he had regard to a range of penalties available to him and set the penalty at the mid-point of the range. He did not identify what the range was.

Although the Regulatory Action Policy states that a panel of non-executive advisers may be convened to make a recommendation on penalty when it is over £1 million, this is not a requirement. It was not done in this case and nor was it done in the Marriott and British Airways cases.

In assessing the amount the Commissioner noted the following:-

- The Commissioner could not identify any specific gain from the infringements. Clearview had refused to provide any information on turnover or income.

- It had offered its services to UK law enforcement agencies on a trial basis and it had not obtained any income from it. The trial had ended and access to the platform from UK IP addresses had been blocked.

- The infringements had continued from 25 May 2018 to 18 May 2022;

- A large number of data subjects resident in the UK were likely to have been affected;

- The processing was invisible and involved special category data;

- The Commissioner's Regulatory Action Policy states that novel or invasive technology causing a high degree of intrusion into the privacy of individuals can expect regulatory action at the "upper end of the scale";

- Although Clearview had previously acted on requests from data subjects to exclude their images from future searches it no longer did so;

- Clearview said that it only offered its services to law enforcement agencies but it had also offered its services to the Government of Ukraine in its war with Russia which was an example of the potential for expanding the scope of the services;

- Clearview ought, at the very least, have been aware that processing the personal data of very substantial numbers of UK data subjects gave rise to a very significant risk that the UK GDPR applied;

- No images of UK subjects had been deleted from the Clearview data base. Personal data continued to be processed in a non-compliant manner and continued to give rise to risks to data subjects;

- Although Clearview's withdrawal from the UK market had lessened the potential impact on UK data subjects. the service continued to be offered to non-UK customers and its data base included UK subjects;

- Clearview had implemented some organisational and technical measures to protect the data that it processed. However there were no measures to bring its processing into compliance with the UK GDPR.

- The Commissioner noted there were no relevant previous infringements and Clearview had responded to the Commissioner's enquiries in timely manner. However the undertaking did not answer all questions and simply restated its position on jurisdiction.

- The incident became known to the commissioner through its own proactive investigation.

An enforcement notice was sent in tandem with the penalty notice. It included the following requirements:

- to delete the personal data of data subjects resident in the UK within 6 months of the expiry of the appeal period;

- to refrain from any further processing of personal data belonging to data subjects resident in UK within three months of the expiry of the appeal period;

It is likely there has been no compliance with these provisions.

When publicising the fine, John Edwards, the Information Commissioner, said:

> *Clearview AI Inc has collected multiple images of people all over the world, including in the UK, from a variety of websites and social media platforms, creating a database with more than 20 billion images. The company not only enables identification of those people, but effectively monitors their behaviour and offers it as a commercial service. That is unacceptable. That is why we have acted to protect people in the UK by both fining the company and issuing an enforcement notice.*
>
> *People expect that their personal information will be respected, regardless of where in the world their data is being used. That is why global companies need international enforcement. Working with colleagues around the world helped us take this action and protect people from such intrusive activity.*

This international cooperation is essential to protect people's privacy rights in 2022. That means working with regulators in other countries, as we did in this case with our Australian colleagues. And it means working with regulators in Europe, which is why I am meeting them in Brussels this week so we can collaborate to tackle global privacy harms.

Tuckers Solicitors – 28 February 2022

Many breaches of security arise from outdated software systems. Tuckers Solicitors were fined £98,000 or 3.25% of annual turnover for June 2020 following a breach of the security requirements of Articles 5 and 32. From 25 May 2018 to 25 August 2020 they failed to process personal data in a secure manner by using appropriate technical or organisational methods.

They suffered a ransomware attack on 24 August 2020 which resulted in the encryption of 972,191 individual files on their archive server, of which 24,712 were court bundles. Sixty of the court bundles were exfiltrated and released onto the dark web. Fifteen of these bundles related to criminal proceedings and the others concerned civil proceedings. All the criminal trials had been concluded. There was a mix of live and archived civil cases. Some of the court bundles were outside the seven year retention period fixed by Tuckers.

The files included personal data which fell into the special category, such as health data and criminal convictions. There was also data relating to children, financial data and information relating to race and ethnic origin.In some cases the data included privileged information between clients and Tuckers. As the Commissioner noted, some of the data *related to individuals that were particularly vulnerable, including children and individuals involved in significant crimes. This, in the Commissioner's view, increases the severity of this infringement, given that this type of data required particularly high levels of security to be applied to it.*

The ICO determined that Tuckers had delayed four months in applying a patch to fix a vulnerability in its software, although the software provider had repeatedly warned that the patch was needed. It did not use Multi Factor Authentication to allow access to its intranet remotely. This was a comparatively low-cost preventative measure which Tuckers should have implemented. It failed to encrypt data. Although the firm failed to meet crucial aspects of the Cyber Essentials accreditation requirements in October 2019, ten months later it had still not resolved this issue.

CHAPTER EIGHT

PROCEDURE FOR APPEALS TO THE TRIBUNAL

Introduction

There are at least two well-worn routes to the First-tier Tribunal (General Regulatory Chamber) (the Tribunal) which deals with appeals against Government regulators. Firstly, a data subject may appeal under section 166 of the Data Protection Act 2018 for an order that the Commissioner progress their complaint. Secondly, a controller or processor may appeal against an information, assessment, enforcement, penalty and penalty variation notice under section 162 of the Act.

Appeals to the Tribunal are governed by the *Tribunal Procedure (First-tier Tribunal) (General Regulatory Chamber) Rules 2009* (as amended) (the Tribunal Rules). There is a right of appeal to the Upper Tribunal under the *Tribunal Procedure (Upper Tribunal) Rules 2008* (the Upper Tribunal Rules). From there a person may appeal to the Court of Appeal under the *Appeals from the Upper Tribunal to the Court of Appeal Order 2008.*

Application to First-tier Tribunal (General Regulatory Chamber) to progress a complaint.

The overriding objective of the Tribunal Rules is to enable the Tribunal to deal with cases *fairly and justly.*[136] In order to achieve this the Tribunal has a very broad discretion as to how it manages cases. It is required to

[136] Rule 2 The Tribunal Procedure (First-tier Tribunal) (General Regulatory Chamber) Rules 2009

deal with them *in ways that are proportionate to the importance of the case, the complexity of the issues, the anticipated costs and the resources of the parties.* The parties are under a duty to help the Tribunal to achieve the overriding objective.

The deadline for lodging any notice of appeal (Form T98 available online for an order to progress a complaint is 28 days from the expiry of six months from the date when the Commissioner received the complaint. [137] The Tribunal has no discretion to extend the deadline. For example, if the commissioner received a complaint on 5 March 2022, the deadline will be 28 days from 5 September 2022 which is 3 October. The Tribunal rules specify the cut off time as 5pm.[138]

There is no court issue fee. Representatives of the parties need not be legally qualified.

Any supporting documents should accompany the appeal notice. If the information is confidential, personal or sensitive this issue maybe raised in the application notice and the information provided separately to the application with an instruction that it should not be shared with other parties. The Tribunal may later make an order prohibiting the disclosure or publication of specified documents or information[139] including to a party to the proceedings.

When completing the application notice an indication needs to be given as to whether the appellant agrees to the appeal being determined on the papers or whether they would like an oral hearing, which may be held on the Cloud Video Platform where appropriate.

---

[137] Rule 22 (6) (f) 9 ibid

[138] Rule 12 (1) ibid

[139] Rule 14 (1) ibid

The Tribunal sends the application notice to the Information Commissioner. The deadline for providing a response is 28 days from receipt.

The appellant may lodge with the Tribunal a reply to the respondent's response, together with any additional document on which they wish to rely.[140] The deadline for lodging a reply is 28 days after receipt of the response. The respondent then has fourteen days from receipt of the reply to provide a list of any further material which might assist the appellant's case as disclosed in the reply.

The Tribunal adopts a flexible approach and generally decides how best to proceed after consulting the parties. It must determine appeals at a hearing either in person or remotely unless the parties consent to it being determined on the papers and the Tribunal is satisfied that it can properly determine the issues without a hearing. [141] It may strike out cases under rule 8 on the papers.

It may give a direction on its own initiative or on the application of the parties. It may admit evidence whether or not it would be admissible in a civil trial. [142] It may summon witnesses to give evidence and/or to produce documents. Similarly it may make costs orders on its own initiative or on an application. It may correct clerical mistakes and accidental slips or omissions in any document produced by it under rule 40. It may also set aside a decision which disposes of proceedings where there have been certain procedural irregularities under rule 41.

An application to appeal must be made within 28 days of the Tribunal sending its decision notice or written reasons if later. On receipt of an application the Tribunal must first consider whether to review its own

---

[140] Rule 28 (1) The Tribunal Procedure (First-tier Tribunal) (General Regulatory Chamber) Rules 2009

[141] Rule 32 ibid

[142] Rule 15 (2) (a) (1) ibid

decision under rule 43. It may review its decision if satisfied that there was an error of law under rule 44. [143]If it decides not to it must consider whether to give permission to appeal. If it refuses the applicant has the right to apply to the Upper Tribunal for leave.

All hearings must be held in public. However, a Tribunal may give a direction that a hearing or part of it is to be held in private.[144] The Tribunal may also determine who is to attend the hearing or part of it.

Where a party fails to comply with a provision of the Tribunal Rules, a practice direction or a direction given by the Tribunal, the Tribunal *may take such action as it considers just* which comprises:-

- waiving the requirement;
- requiring the failure to be remedied;
- striking out the case;
- referring the matter to the Upper Tribunal under section 25 of the *Tribunals, Courts and Enforcement Act 2007* (which covers *inter alia* the attendance of witnesses and the production of documents); or
- barring or restricting a party's participation in the proceedings.[145]

[143] Rule 44 (1) (b) ibid

[144] Rule 35 (2) ibid

[145] Rule 7 (3) the Tribunal Procedure (First-tier Tribunal) (General Regulatory Chamber) Rules 2009

A party's case will be struck out in a number of circumstances identified by Rule 8. Most importantly, it will be struck out if *the Tribunal considers there is no reasonable prospect the appellant's case, or part of it succeeding.* [146]

In practice the Commissioner is likely to remedy any failure to progress a complaint under section 166 when he receives the issued application notice. If the data subject wishes to progress their appeal in any event the Tribunal is likely to ask the individual for representations as to why the appeal should not be struck out. [147] These representations will probably be requested in writing. The case may then be struck out without a hearing by either a Registrar or a Tribunal judge.[148]

A registrar's decision to strike out can be considered afresh by a judge under rule 4 (3) Tribunal Rules. An appellant may apply to reinstate proceedings that have been struck out under rule 8 (5). The application must be made in writing no more than 28 days after receipt of the notice striking out the case.

Costs do not follow the event. The Tribunal may make an order for costs on its own initiative or on an application where a party *has acted unreasonably in bringing, defending or conducting the proceedings.* [149] An order may be made against the Information Commissioner if it considers the decision, direction or order he made that is the subject of the appeal was unreasonable. Any application for costs must be made no later than 14 days after the date when the Tribunal sent a decision notice disposing of the proceedings. An order for costs cannot be made without first allowing the paying party the opportunity to make representations.

---

[146] Rule 8 (3) (c) ibid

[147] Rules 8 (3) (c) and 8 (4) ibid.

[148] Rule 32 (3) ibid

[149] Rule 10 (b) ibid

Appeal to Upper Tribunal (Administrative Appeals Chamber)

The procedure for appeals to the Upper Tribunal broadly mirrors the procedure for appeals to the Tribunal. It has a broad discretion so as to achieve the overriding objective of dealing with cases *fairly and justly.*

Before making any application for leave to appeal to the Upper Tribunal, an application must first be made to the Tribunal and refused. The deadline for making a renewed application to the Upper Tribunal is one month after the Tribunal gave notice of its decision to refuse permission to appeal. [150]

Under section 11 (1) *Tribunals Courts and Enforcement Act 2007,* an appeal to the Upper Tribunal lies only on *any point of law arising from a decision* of the Tribunal. The error of law must be material in that it must have affected the outcome of the case in some material way. The Upper Tribunal will give permission to appeal only if there is a realistic prospect of success, unless exceptionally there is some other good reason to do so.

In *Smith v Cosworth Casting Processes Limited* [1997] 1 WLR 1538 Lord Woolf refused to grant leave to appeal where the court was satisfied that appellant had no realistic prospect of success, which was the same as the *no arguable case* test, with *realistic* being adopted to show that a merely fanciful prospect or unrealistic argument was insufficient. However, where it was in the public interest or clarification of legal issues was required, the application could be granted even if the test was not satisfied.

The Upper Tribunal helpfully gave some examples in plain English of where the Tribunal might go wrong in law in *Lindsay Fraser v ICO* HA - 2022 – 001546. The examples were where the Tribunal:

a) Did not apply the correct law or wrongly interpreted the law;

[150] Rule 21 (2) and (3) Tribunal Procedure (Upper Tribunal) Rules 2008

b) Made a procedural error;

c) Had no evidence, or not enough evidence, to support its decision;

d) Failed to find sufficient facts; or

e) Did not give adequate reasons.

In this case the application to appeal was found to be *utterly devoid of even the faintest glimmer of merit* .

Where the Upper Tribunal grants permission to appeal there will not usually be any need to lodge a separate appeal bundle. The parties make written submissions which are copied to each other. There are no fees for an appeal.

The Upper Tribunal aims to deal with applications for leave to appeal within ten weeks. It aims to deal with appeals within 20 weeks of permission to appeal being granted.

Under section 12 (2) (a) and (b) (i) of the Upper Tribunal Rules, the Upper Tribunal may set aside a decision of the Tribunal and remit it to a new tribunal for consideration.

Most cases are decided on the papers. Parties may request an oral hearing at both the application and the appeal stages. Hearings must be in public unless the judge directs otherwise.

Totally Without Merit

> *Where the Upper Tribunal considers the whole or part of an application to be totally without merit, it shall record that fact in its decision notice and, in these circumstances, the person seeking permission may not request the decision or part of the decision (as the case may be) to be reconsidered at a hearing:*

rule 22 (4A) Tribunal Procedure (Upper Tribunal) Rules 2008, with effect from 6 April 2022:

Totally without merit means bound to fail (see *R (Grace) v SSHD* [2014] 1 WLR 3432).

CHAPTER NINE

ENFORCEMENT BY DATA SUBJECTS IN THE COURTS

Introduction

Perhaps surprisingly, an individual need not be a data subject in order to bring a claim for compensation in the courts. [151] Any person who has suffered damage as a result of a breach of the data protection legislation may claim by issuing proceedings in the High Court or County Court. The cause of action is a statutory tort and lies against a data processor as well as a controller. Both appear to owe the world at large a duty to comply with the data protection legislation.

Damage is defined as *financial loss and damage not involving financial loss such as distress.* [152] It is only in rare cases that pecuniary loss is proved. The definition may broad enough to cover damage to reputation per se. In any event it is likely to cover distress arising from reputational damage resulting from a breach.

A processor is only liable for damage where it has not complied with an obligation under the data protection legislation specifically directed at processors, such as the Article 32 security requirements, or where it has acted outside or contrary to the processor's lawful instructions. [153]

Not only may a data subject make a claim for compensation, they may also apply to the court for a compliance order requiring the controller or

---

[151] Section 169 DPA 2018

[152] Section 169 (5) ibid

[153] Section 169 (2) ibid

processor to rectify any infringement of their rights under the UK GDPR or Data Protection Act 2018. [154] For example, a court may order that access be given to the claimant's personal data by a given deadline, in addition to or instead of making an award of compensation.

Needless to say, both controllers and processors may raise a complete defence to any claim for compensation if they can prove they were not in any way responsible for the event giving rise to the damage.[155]

In a case where controllers, and/or processors are involved in the same processing, and they are responsible for any breach of the data protection legislation which causes an individual damage, the individual's rights may be exercised against any one or all of them. Each may claim a contribution from others responsible to any compensation they pay the data subject.[156]

Where there are numerous claimants against the same defendants arising out of the same alleged breaches, proceedings are likely to be issued in the High Court, and a Group Litigation Order may be obtained.

Causes of action

The processing of personal data may give rise to a number of causes of action in the civil courts, in addition to a cause of action for breach of the data protection legislation. These are generally pleaded in the alternative.

Possible causes of action include:

[154] Section 167 ibid

[155] Section 169 ibid

[156] Article 82(4) and (5) UK GDPR

- Breach of the right to privacy under Article 8 Human Rights Act 1998;
- Misuse of private information (a distinct tort);
- Breach of confidence (a distinct tort);
- Judicial review.

Where liability is established under more than once cause of action, the court is careful to avoid double recovery for the same loss or damage. It is important to appreciate that misuse of private information can give rise to damages for loss of control over a person's information without more. In other words the breach itself is compensatable. Damages for this may be recovered in addition to any damages awarded for distress and/or financial loss.

Since the first data protection principle requires that data be processed lawfully, any unlawfulness in relation to data processing will breach this principle, irrespective of whether there has been a breach of the data protection legislation.

High Court or county court

Depending on the value of the claim a person may issue in the High Court or the county court. The High Court is generally reserved for claims for damages exceeding £100,000, save where a case is complex and/or of general public importance. Since the value of individual data claims is generally low, most are issued in the cunty court which means there is little binding authority. In any event awards of damages awards are very fact sensitive.

Advice from Commissioner

If a claimant has made an earlier complaint before resorting to proceedings, the Commissioner may have expressed a view on whether the data protection legislation has been breached. An indication that there has been a breach is likely to encourage the claimant and may be persuasive in the court proceedings. However, the judge may reach a different conclusion.

Application for assistance from Commissioner in special purposes proceedings

The Commissioner may give financial assistance to a party (claimant or defendant) in special purposes proceedings. [157] The ICO website confirms that no legal help will be provided if the personal data was used for anything other than special purposes. This echoes the Commissioner's power, described in Chapter 2, to make a written determination that personal data is not being processed *only* for special purposes and so special purposes restrictions do not apply. [158]

The possible assistance includes payment of legal costs and indemnifying the applicant for any liability to pay costs, expenses or damages in connection with the proceedings. The Commissioner may also give advice.

Any application for assistance is made under section 175 (1) DPA 2018. It will not be granted unless the Commissioner considers *the case involves a matter of substantial public importance.*[159] The Commissioner's website confirms: *This is likely to be where there has been, or there could be, a serious infringement causing substantial damage or distress to an individual, or*

---

[157] Section 175 DPA 2018

[158] Section 174 (3) ibid

[159] Section 175 (3) ibid

where the outcome of the case might significantly affect the interpretation of data protection law... He expects very few cases will be eligible for assistance.

When deciding not to provide assistance the Commissioner must notify the applicant of this as soon as reasonably practicable, giving reasons for his decision.

When he does provide assistance, the Commissioner has first charge on any costs a successful applicant recovers on the conclusion of proceedings. There is no mention of any charge on compensation.. However, there is a charge on any sum payable as part of an out of court settlement.

Stay of special purposes proceedings

In provisions designed to protect freedom of expression by preventing data protection law from being used to obstruct publication, the court must stay any special purposes proceedings. [160] The stay must remain in place until the Commissioner makes a determination that the personal data is not being processed only for special purposes or until the claim is withdrawn.[161]

Claims against the media

A data subject who wishes to claim compensation against the media should consider the IMPRSS and IPSO arbitration schemes before issuing proceedings.

[160] Section 176 (1) DPA 2018

[161] Section 176 (3) ibid

Group litigation orders – opt in

In a case involving many claimants or defendants a Group Litigation Order may be obtained under CPR rule 19. 22. Rule 19.21 provides:

> *Group Litigation Order ('GLO') means an order made under rule 19.22 to provide for the case management of claims which give rise to common or related issues of fact or law (the 'GLO issues').*

Where a GLO is made, claims arising out of the same breaches are generally transferred to a managing court after issue, entered onto the GLO register and managed together by a single dedicated judge. One or more of the claims are selected to be tried as test claims while the others are stayed pending the outcome. The GLO may be publicised in order to encourage those affected to join the proceedings.

The first Group Litigation Order in a data breach case was the British Airways Data Event Group Litigation Order made on 4 October 2019, arising out of the security breaches described in the preceding chapter.

Claimants are often reluctant to opt in and join such proceedings, particularly where the amount recovered is likely to be small. Only 16,000 out of more than 400,000 effected by the breach issued proceedings against British Airways so many failed to recover compensation even though they were entitled to it.

Furthermore the issue and administration of such claims is expensive. Evidence, including witness statements, must be obtained from each individual to support their claim. Consequently group litigation is often uneconomic and such cases tend to settle. The British Airways case settled after mediation, on terms that were confidential.

A data breach case that did not settle and went to the Supreme Court was *WM Morrison Supermarkets plc v Various Claimants*[2020] UKSC 12. Was Morrisons vicariously liable for the actions of a disgruntled employee who released the personal data of nearly 100,000 fellow employees onto the internet? The data included name, address, gender, DOB, phone number, NI number, bank sorting code, bank account number and salary. The employee was later convicted of several offences in relation to the disclosure and sentenced to eight years imprisonment.

Only about 10,000 of the effected employees issued proceedings against Morrisons for breach of the Data Protection Act 1998, misuse of private information and breach of confidence. They claimed compensation for distress and anxiety. A Group Litigation Order was made and ten test claimants were selected to proceed to a liability only trial.

The High Court and Court of Appeal both decided that Morrisons was vicariously liable for the criminal actions of its employee in all three causes of action, including beach of the Data Protection Act 1998. They rejected the argument that the employee had assumed the role of data controller when he copied the information onto his own USB stick and released it online. The disclosures were carried out in the course of his employment as an in house auditor. Morrisons had provided him with the personal data so that he could disclose it to Morrisons' auditors. His disclosure of the information on the internet in addition was closely connected to his duties.

The Supreme Court disagreed. What was highly relevant was whether the disgruntled employee had been acting on his employer's business or for his own personal reasons. He had been acting for his own personal reasons in order to harm his employer. Unsurprisingly, the Supreme Court knew of no cases *in which it has been argued that an employer might be vicariously liable for wrongdoing which was designed specifically to harm the employer.* Morrisons avoided liability and the claimants recovered nothing.

Representative actions – opt out

CPR 19.8 provides that a claim may be initiated or continued by or against one or more persons as representatives of others who have the *same interest* in the claim. Representative actions are easier and less costly to manage than cases where a Group Litigation Order is made. An individual need not issue proceedings in order to be part of the case. They are automatically opted in, and there is no need to obtain evidence to support an individual's case.

Lloyd v Google LLC [2021] UKSC 50

In 2018 a single claimant applied for leave to serve proceedings outside the jurisdiction on Google Inc in California. He alleged that for several months in late 2011 and early 2012, Google had secretly tracked the internet activity of millions of Apple iPhone users (known as the *Safari Workaround*) and used the data collected in this way for commercial purposes without their consent. He made the application on his own behalf and also on behalf of four million other unidentified iPhone users in England and Wales. He maintained that they were all entitled to compensation under the Data Protection Act 1998, although the claimant did not plead any particulars of damage.

The claimant relied on Rule 19.8 CPR. However, he accepted that could not use this procedure to claim compensation on behalf of other iPhone users if the compensation recoverable by each user would have to be individually assessed.

He argued that as matter of law compensation can be awarded under DPA 1998 for *loss of control* of personal data without the need to prove that the claimant suffered any financial loss or mental distress as a result of the breach. A figure of £750 was advanced in the letter of claim, which would produce a global award of £3 billion.

The Supreme Court overturned a decision of the Court of Appeal, that had in turn allowed an appeal from the High Court, and confirmed that a claim could not be brought under the DPA 1998 simply for an infringement of the DPA's provisions. There had to be proof of damage such as distress or financial loss. The court needed to consider liability and quantum in individual cases. A representative action in which claimants were required to opt out was not appropriate for this type of claim.

However, the Supreme Court raised the possibility of a split trial and establishing liability as a representative action. If liability were established the result could be publicised and claimants encouraged to opt into a class action to recover damages. More claimants were likely to join once liability had been determined in their favour in the representative action.

However, this approach did not solve difficulties with litigation funding. Would legal expenses insurers be able to recover their costs of the liability only trial?

Another possibility the Supreme Court suggested was to consider a representative action for misuse of private information only. This would mean claiming damages for the breach only , that is the loss of control of personal information without claiming compensation for distress and other financial loss. User damages could be recovered on the basis of a hypothetical fee payable to each individual for using their information.

This is likely to be explored in the future.

Compensation cases

Cases decided before 25 May 2018 and the implementation of the GDPR and Data Protection Act 2018 continue to provide guidance on the level of damages recovered for *distress.*

Halliday v Creation Credit Finance Limited [2013] EWCA Civ 33 CA Arden LJ

Creation Credit Finance Limited provided Equifax, the credit rating agency, with inaccurate information showing the claimant in arrears with his payments over a period of eight months, without any agreement from the credit provider. Judgement in default was entered for the claimant, and nominal damages were awarded without fixing any amount. The judge decided there was insufficient evidence of damage to reputation or credit, and declined to hear the claim for distress.

The claimant appealed against the award of damages. In a rather elliptical judgement the Court of Appeal held that the claimant's evidence did not establish damage to reputation or credit. The breach had been limited and there had been no malicious or fraudulent intent on the part of the defendant. The breach had arisen from a single technical error. The judge noted there was:

- *No contemporaneous evidence of any manifestation of injury to feelings and distress apart from what one would normally expect from frustration.*

- *It is not the intention of the legislation to produce some kind of substantial award. It is intended to be compensation.*

The claimant received £750 compensation for distress.

AB V Ministry of Justice [2014] EWHC 1847 QB Jeremy Baker J

Following the death of his wife, the claimant made several subject access requests to the Ministry of Justice. There were extended delays in responding. It took six years to provide some of the personal data.

The claimant was a professional man who spent a considerable amount of time and expense in obtaining disclosure. He did not quantify the time and expense of securing compliance with his rights of access. The judge awarded nominal damages of £1.00 for the breach of his right of access.

Damages for distress as a result of the breach were difficult to quantify. He had suffered far reaching distress caused by factors other than the infringement of his rights by the delay, including the death of his wife, and the contents of some of the disclosed material.

The judge observed:-

> *... it does seem to me to be of relevance that a more focused approach by the claimant at an earlier stage may have achieved a more directed and swifter disclosure of at least some of this material. In that it appears to have been following a more focused enquiry in relation to this material, during the course of mediation, that the disclosed material was provided to the claimant; albeit after a delay of some months, and of course in the absence of the item of withheld material which ought also to have been disclosed.*
>
> *...I have no medical evidence before me, over and above some items within the correspondence exhibited to the claimant's witness statement, about his state of health and certainly none which deals separately with the contribution which this aspect of delay may have had upon his level of distress. I am also conscious of the claimant's evidence that the main aims of these proceedings has not only been to establish that the defendant has failed to deal with his requests in a timely manner, but to seek the destruction of the disclosed and withheld material; aims which he has now achieved...*

Doing the best he could on the evidence the judge awarded £2,500 for distress caused by the delays.

TLT and others v Secretary of State for the Home Department [2016] EWHC 2217 (QB) Mitting J

The claimants were applicants for asylum whose personal details were mistakenly published by the Home Office on its website on 15 October 2013. The information was contained in a spreadsheet alongside official family returns process statistics, and included name, age, nationality, whether an application for asylum had been made and the stage reached in the family returns process. The general area where the claimant lived could also be inferred. The mistake was discovered on 28 October 2013 when the webpage was immediately taken down.

The defendant accepted there had been breaches of the Data Protection Act 1998 and misuse of private and confidential information. It was also accepted that damages were recoverable for distress at common law for misuse of private information, as well as under the DPA.

The parties agreed that the judge should take into account awards made for psychiatric or psychological injury in personal injury cases to ensure that any award for distress was not out of kilter with them.

The claimants argued that guidance could be derived from cases involving the deliberate dissemination of private and confidential information for gain by media publishers or individuals such as Max Clifford. The judge observed:-

> *In the case of all claimants they maintain that they were deeply shocked and put in fear by the Home Office's error. Their cases are far closer to cases in which claimants have been caused to suffer psychiatric injury by an actionable wrong, whether a careless act or a deliberate wrong, such as child sex abuse.*

Damages could be awarded in respect of loss of control of personal and confidential information, as settled by *Gulati* (below). This would be taken into account when assessing the award but it was neither necessary or desirable to make a separate award under this head.

Various awards were made, including £12,500 for distress in two of the cases, which was not out of kilter with awards for moderate and psychological damage.

Andrea Brown and Commissioner of Police for the Metropolis and Chief Constable of Greater Manchester Police and Greater Manchester Police (Central London County Court, July 2016) – HHJ LUBA QC

The claimant was an officer with the Metropolitan Police who travelled to Barbados with her daughter when she was absent on sick leave. As part of an investigation into possible disciplinary proceedings, the force obtained evidence from the National Border Targeting Centre operated by Greater Manchester Police that confirmed her trip with dates. The Metropolitan Police also obtained information form the airline, which included personal data belonging to her daughter. The claimant argued the information was obtained in breach of her data protection rights since it had been obtained from third parties by the police through channels they used to prevent and detect crime although no crime had been committed. Furthermore, GMP had provided information covering all her flights in the past six years, together with details of her companions, although this was not required.

There was no lawful basis for the processing and both defendants conceded there had been a breach of the Data Protection Act 1998. The judge held that the claimant's right to privacy under Article 8 of the European Convention had also been infringed. In addition there had been a tortious invasion of her privacy.

The claimant unsuccessfully claimed damages for depression. Her evidence that "the whole situation has had a hugely adverse effect on my health" was found to be a gross exaggeration.

However, the judge accepted that she was *totally shocked, upset and angry* as a result of learning of the Metropolitan Police's actions and she was to a lesser extent and at a much later stage *very upset and angry* and d*istressed* about the breach by GMP.

When deciding on the level of compensation the claimant suggested the judge adopt the £10,000 starting point used in the breach of privacy phone hacking case of *Gulati and others v MGN Limited* [2015] EWHC 1482 (Ch). However his case was distinguished since it involved the repeated misuse and abuse of personal data and the disclosure of highly personal material for gain, for wider distribution or with the intent to embarrass.

The claimant recovered £9,000 including compensation for distress caused by the breaches of the Data Protection Act 1998 and Human Rights Act 1998 (which did not add to the value of the claim for distress under the DPA).

She was awarded an additional amount for loss of control of her information as a result of the tortious invasion of her privacy. In *Gulati* Arden LJ reasoned that privacy is a fundamental right, and that loss of control over that privacy is a form of damage for which compensation could be awarded. The loss of control of information meant the information was no longer private, although the amount recovered might have been reduced if the information had been public knowledge anyway. As it was in *Brown*, the dissemination of the information had been limited and it was of a nature that the claimant would probably have provided had she been asked.

Damages were apportioned 2/3:1/3 between the Metropolitan Police and Greater Manchester Police.

There was a claim for aggravated damages which failed.

CHAPTER TEN

CONCLUSION

As data protection law increases in importance so does enforcement, which is a complex area encompassing both regulatory compliance and court proceedings. The regulator is concerned mainly with larger organisations and how their actions, or lack of action, target or impact vulnerable individuals. He has the power to impose large fines that hurt, whatever the size of the organisation.

Individuals in their turn have effective causes of action against the organisations that process their personal data. Although the value of their individual claims may be relatively low, when taken together the overall outlay in damages and costs to many claimants may be significant, triggering early settlement.

In order to reduce the legal costs of proceedings there are likely to be other attempts to recover compensation for millions of data subjects by way of representative actions, perhaps for breach of confidence, in tandem with alleged breaches of the data protection legislation. Where breach of confidence is established, a breach of the first data protection principle of lawful processing inevitably follows.

If and when such an attempt is successful, any fine may pale into insignificance when compared with compensation paid to individuals.

'A Practical Guide to Bad Character Evidence for Criminal Practitioners by Aparna Rao
'A Practical Guide to Extradition Law post-Brexit' by Myles Grandison et al
'A Practical Guide to Hoarding and Mental Health for Housing Lawyers' by Rachel Coyle
'A Practical Guide to Psychiatric Claims in Personal Injury – 2nd Edition' by Liam Ryan
'Stephens on Contractual Indemnities' by Richard Stephens
'A Practical Guide to the EU Succession Regulation' by Richard Frimston
'A Practical Guide to Solicitor and Client Costs – 2nd Edition' by Robin Dunne
'Constructive Dismissal – Practice Pointers and Principles' by Benjimin Burgher
'A Practical Guide to Religion and Belief Discrimination Claims in the Workplace' by Kashif Ali
'A Practical Guide to the Law of Medical Treatment Decisions' by Ben Troke
'Fundamental Dishonesty and QOCS in Personal Injury Proceedings: Law and Practice' by Jake Rowley
'A Practical Guide to the Law in Relation to School Exclusions' by Charlotte Hadfield & Alice de Coverley
'A Practical Guide to Divorce for the Silver Separators' by Karin Walker
'The Right to be Forgotten – The Law and Practical Issues' by Melissa Stock
'A Practical Guide to Planning Law and Rights of Way in National Parks, the Broads and AONBs' by James Maurici QC, James Neill et al
'A Practical Guide to Election Law' by Tom Tabori
'A Practical Guide to the Law in Relation to Surrogacy' by Andrew Powell
'A Practical Guide to Claims Arising from Fatal Accidents – 2nd Edition' by James Patience
'A Practical Guide to the Ownership of Employee Inventions – From Entitlement to Compensation' by James Tumbridge & Ashley Roughton
'A Practical Guide to Asbestos Claims' by Jonathan Owen & Gareth McAloon
'A Practical Guide to Stamp Duty Land Tax in England and Northern Ireland' by Suzanne O'Hara
'A Practical Guide to the Law of Farming Partnerships' by Philip Whitcomb
'Covid-19, Homeworking and the Law – The Essential Guide to Employment and GDPR Issues' by Forbes Solicitors
'Covid-19 and Criminal Law – The Essential Guide' by Ramya Nagesh

'Covid-19 and Family Law in England and Wales – The Essential Guide' by Safda Mahmood
'A Practical Guide to the Law of Unlawful Eviction and Harassment – 2nd Edition' by Stephanie Lovegrove
'Covid-19, Brexit and the Law of Commercial Leases – The Essential Guide' by Mark Shelton
'A Practical Guide to Costs in Personal Injury Claims – 2nd Edition' by Matthew Hoe
'A Practical Guide to the General Data Protection Regulation (GDPR) – 2nd Edition' by Keith Markham
'Ellis on Credit Hire – Sixth Edition' by Aidan Ellis & Tim Kevan
'A Practical Guide to Working with Litigants in Person and McKenzie Friends in Family Cases' by Stuart Barlow
'Protecting Unregistered Brands: A Practical Guide to the Law of Passing Off' by Lorna Brazell
'A Practical Guide to Secondary Liability and Joint Enterprise Post-Jogee' by Joanne Cecil & James Mehigan
'A Practical Guide to the Pre-Action RTA Claims Protocol for Personal Injury Lawyers' by Antonia Ford
'A Practical Guide to Neighbour Disputes and the Law' by Alexander Walsh
'A Practical Guide to Forfeiture of Leases' by Mark Shelton
'A Practical Guide to Coercive Control for Legal Practitioners and Victims' by Rachel Horman
'A Practical Guide to Rights Over Airspace and Subsoil' by Daniel Gatty
'Tackling Disclosure in the Criminal Courts – A Practitioner's Guide' by Narita Bahra QC & Don Ramble
'A Practical Guide to the Law of Driverless Cars – Second Edition' by Alex Glassbrook, Emma Northey & Scarlett Milligan
'A Practical Guide to TOLATA Claims' by Greg Williams
'A Practical Guide to Elderly Law – 2nd Edition' by Justin Patten
'A Practical Guide to Responding to Housing Disrepair and Unfitness Claims' by Iain Wightwick
'A Practical Guide to the Construction and Rectification of Wills and Trust Instruments' by Edward Hewitt
'A Practical Guide to the Law of Bullying and Harassment in the Workplace' by Philip Hyland

'How to Be a Freelance Solicitor: A Practical Guide to the SRA-Regulated Freelance Solicitor Model' by Paul Bennett
'A Practical Guide to Prison Injury Claims' by Malcolm Johnson
'A Practical Guide to the Small Claims Track - 2nd Edition' by Dominic Bright
'A Practical Guide to Advising Clients at the Police Station' by Colin Stephen McKeown-Beaumont
'A Practical Guide to Antisocial Behaviour Injunctions' by Iain Wightwick
'Practical Mediation: A Guide for Mediators, Advocates, Advisers, Lawyers, and Students in Civil, Commercial, Business, Property, Workplace, and Employment Cases' by Jonathan Dingle with John Sephton
'The Mini-Pupillage Workbook' by David Boyle
'A Practical Guide to Crofting Law' by Brian Inkster
'A Practical Guide to Spousal Maintenance' by Liz Cowell
'A Practical Guide to the Law of Domain Names and Cybersquatting' by Andrew Clemson
'A Practical Guide to the Law of Gender Pay Gap Reporting' by Harini Iyengar
'NHS Whistleblowing and the Law' by Joseph England
'Employment Law and the Gig Economy' by Nigel Mackay & Annie Powell
'A Practical Guide to Noise Induced Hearing Loss (NIHL) Claims' by Andrew Mckie, Ian Skeate, Gareth McAloon
'An Introduction to Beauty Negligence Claims – A Practical Guide for the Personal Injury Practitioner' by Greg Almond
'Intercompany Agreements for Transfer Pricing Compliance' by Paul Sutton
'Zen and the Art of Mediation' by Martin Plowman
'A Practical Guide to the SRA Principles, Individual and Law Firm Codes of Conduct 2019 – What Every Law Firm Needs to Know' by Paul Bennett
'A Practical Guide to Adoption for Family Lawyers' by Graham Pegg
'A Practical Guide to Industrial Disease Claims' by Andrew Mckie & Ian Skeate
'A Practical Guide to Redundancy' by Philip Hyland
'A Practical Guide to Vicarious Liability' by Mariel Irvine
'A Practical Guide to Applications for Landlord's Consent and Variation of Leases' by Mark Shelton
'A Practical Guide to Relief from Sanctions Post-Mitchell and Denton' by Peter Causton

www.ingramcontent.com/pod-product-compliance
Ingram Content Group UK Ltd.
Pitfield, Milton Keynes, MK11 3LW, UK
UKHW020147290926
15471UKWH00004B/741

9 781914 608407